Stocks Under Rocks

STOCKS UNDER ROCKS

How to Uncover Overlooked, Profitable Market Opportunities

Peter Ricchiuti

with
Annette Naake Sisco

Vice President, Publisher: Tim Moore
Associate Publisher and Director of Marketing: Amy Neidlinger
Operations Specialist: Jodi Kemper
Cover Designer: Alan Clements
Managing Editor: Kristy Hart
Project Editor: Andy Beaster
Copy Editor: Sarah Kearns
Proofreader: Debbie Williams
Indexer: Cheryl Lenser
Compositor: Gloria Schurick
Manufacturing Buyer: Dan Uhrig

FT Press offers excellent discounts on this book when ordered in quantity for bulk purchases or special sales. For more information, please contact U.S. Corporate and Government Sales, 1-800-382-3419, corpsales@pearsontechgroup.com. For sales outside the U.S., please contact International Sales at international@pearsoned.com.

Company and product names mentioned herein are the trademarks or registered trademarks of their respective owners.

ISBN-10: 0-13-339909-5
ISBN-13: 978-0-13-339909-7

Pearson Education LTD.
Pearson Education Australia PTY, Limited.
Pearson Education Singapore, Pte. Ltd.
Pearson Education Asia, Ltd.
Pearson Education Canada, Ltd.
Pearson Educación de Mexico, S.A. de C.V.
Pearson Education—Japan
Pearson Education Malaysia, Pte. Ltd.

Library of Congress Control Number: 2013950510

I dedicate this book to my wonderful wife, Laurie,
with gratitude for your love and patience,
and to my sons, Matthew and William,
who keep me laughing and have made me a proud dad.

Contents

Acknowledgments

Thanks to the Burkenroad Reports team here at Tulane. Marie Daigle, Jennifer Smith, Anthony Wood, Lesley Baker, Pam Shaw, and Robert Morton have been innovative, patient, and tireless. Additionally, I'd like to thank Tim Banfell for his creative input, and our travel coordinator, Wendell Fjeld.

I would also like to thank the deans who have supported both me and the program for all these years: James McFarland, Angelo DiNisi, and Ira Solomon.

A special thanks to Gary Fishman of Anreder & Co. I met Gary while giving a talk for a Tulane admissions program, and he thought I should write a book about our course. Over the years, several people have suggested a book, but Gary had a very nice way of "nudging" me to make it happen.

I am especially grateful to the late Aaron Selber of Shreveport, Louisiana, and the entire Burkenroad family for their continued generosity and encouragement through both bull and bear markets.

Aaron, one of the most successful investors I've ever met, taught me a lot over the years. He and his wife, Peggy Burkenroad Selber, have been the primary benefactors of the Burkenroad Reports program. I came to rely on Aaron's wisdom and counsel on matters both personal and professional.

Aaron and Peggy Selber at the head table of the 16th Annual Burkenroad Reports Investment Conference (April, 2012).

And last but far from least, thanks to Scott Cowen, president of Tulane University from 1998 to 2014. His dedication to excellence in the face of some of our region's most challenging times has been an inspiration. It has been a true honor to work on his team.

About the Authors

Peter Ricchiuti lives in New Orleans with his wife and two sons. He teaches courses on finance and investments at Tulane University's A.B. Freeman School of Business and also hosts the weekly business program "Out to Lunch" on the local NPR affiliate, WWNO. Peter provides surprisingly entertaining addresses to dozens of groups throughout the country each year on economics and the financial markets.

Annette Naake Sisco is a New Orleans-based writer and the features editor for *The New Orleans Advocate.*

Introduction

I wrote this book because I wanted to encourage individual investors to trust their own stock-picking abilities. Along the way, I hope to bust a few Wall Street myths and share some levity.

Why should you listen to what I have to say? Well, first of all, I have a lot of great stories to tell. Secondly, I've been in the investing business for almost 35 years, the past 27 of them teaching courses in finance at Tulane University in New Orleans, where I am founder and director of the Burkenroad Reports student stock research program. I graduated from Babson College and started my career in the Boston office of the old-line investment banking firm of Kidder Peabody & Co. After that, I served for more than five years as the assistant state treasurer and chief investment officer for the state of Louisiana, managing the state's $3 billion investment portfolio and serving on boards overseeing another $8 billion in retirement funds.

I came to teach full-time at Tulane University in New Orleans in 1993. Tulane is a highly selective research university founded in 1834. Since reopening just one semester after Hurricane Katrina hit in 2005, I've been calling Tulane University the "greatest comeback since Lazarus." Still, I'm glad that the university didn't accept my motto suggestion in 2004: "Tulane University—Higher Education Below Sea Level."

Over the past few years, we have averaged about 35,000 applications for just 1,700 freshman openings every fall. The A.B. Freeman School of Business, in the center of Tulane's leafy Uptown campus, is highly ranked (our finance department was named one of the world's ten best by *The Financial Times*), and is currently celebrating its 100th anniversary.

Besides teaching, I host a popular business program called "Out to Lunch" on the National Public Radio affiliate here in New Orleans. Post-Katrina, New Orleans is a much more vibrant business community. *Forbes* called the city "America's New Frontier for Business Opportunity," and Under 30 CEO (http://www.Under30CEO.com) recently named New Orleans the "#1 City for Young Entrepreneurs." Each week I bring two entrepreneurs to the famous Commander's Palace restaurant and interview them about their successful, often surprising, business ideas.

Over the last 30 years, I have spoken about the financial markets to more than 1,000 groups in 47 states, with audiences as diverse as nuns, water park owners, investment managers, and the New Orleans Saints. I taught these NFL players in investment workshops. (And, contrary to popular belief, I was not behind the Saints financial bounty scandal of 2012!)

In 1993, I received a generous grant from the Louisiana Education Quality Trust Fund, and later that year, I founded what has become known as the Burkenroad Reports stock research program at the A.B. Freeman School of Business (www.burkenroad.org). The program is named in honor of William B. Burkenroad Jr., an alumnus and long-time supporter of Tulane's business school.

For Burkenroad Reports, my smart young army of student analysts combs six Southern states to get the "skinny" on underfollowed public companies. This is the first student stock research program in the country where students actually meet with top management, visit company sites, develop financial models, and publish investment research reports on little-known companies with outstanding potential. These are the stocks under rocks—dozens of companies that Wall Street has more or less ignored to its own peril.

Since the beginning, each student has been required to sign an agreement not to purchase stock in any of the individual companies followed by Burkenroad Reports until after they've graduated. It's also our policy to prohibit my staff and myself from making such purchases. We actually implemented these rules years before Wall Street put into place similar restrictions on its analysts forbidding them from buying shares in the companies they follow. To us here at Burkenroad, this seemed like a Sunday-school-simple example of avoiding a conflict of interest.

Our research impressed Hancock Bank of Mississippi so much, it started a mutual fund built around the program. These student-produced research reports help power this fund that began on December 31, 2001 and has outperformed about 99 percent of all stock mutual funds over nearly a dozen years. Since its inception, the Hancock Horizon Burkenroad Small Cap Fund (Ticker Symbols: HYBUX & HHBUX) has chalked up a 271% total rate of return, double that of the small cap Russell 2000 (+132%) and more than three times the S&P 500's +77% return. The fund has more than $400 million in assets and is managed by David Lundgren at Hancock Bank.

Burkenroad Fund (HYBUX) vs. S&P 500 Index vs. Russell 2000 Index

Range 12/31/2001	- 06/28/2013		Period Monthly	No. of Period	138 Month(s)
Security	Currency	Price Change	Total Return	Difference	Annual Eq
1. SPX Index	USD	39.91%	77.25%	-193.33%	5.10%
2. HYBUX US Equity	USD	221.33%	270.59%		12.07%
3. RTY Index	USD	100.10%	132.13%	-138.46%	7.60%

The Burkenroad Reports Course

Each year, I take 200 students, break them up into teams of five, and assign each team to research one of 40 small to mid-sized, under-followed public companies headquartered in Louisiana, Texas,

Mississippi, Alabama, Georgia, and Florida. (I know, pretty much the financial center of the country—NOT.)

We don't just track these businesses on paper. We strap on hard hats or pull on rubber boots, tour the plants, and meet the CEOs, CFOs, and other company decision makers. We have the best field trips in the free world. We've flown out to and visited offshore oil rigs, toured steel mills, and walked through chicken processing plants. If you've never been to a chicken processing plant, do take the family!

I got the itch for visiting companies when I was at Kidder Peabody & Co. in the early 1980s and we were doing a secondary offering on a company that bred hairless rats for medical research. Our bosses thought we could do a better job talking to clients about the deal if we actually visited with the company and saw what they did. They put us on a bus, and when we arrived, we were told to put on germ-free smocks, pants, booties, and gloves. (I asked why and was told that a group of previous visitors had brought germs, and, well, the rats died.) I was fascinated. And so were all my colleagues on the trip. It was a big-boy Mister Rogers episode come to life!

You may have heard of Burkenroad Reports, since the program has been featured in *The Wall Street Journal, The New York Times, CNBC, CNN,* and *PBS's Nightly Business Report,* among other places

Here's another reason you should take the time to read this book. This is a great time for individuals to research and invest in stocks, particularly under-followed stocks. Yet frankly, I've never seen people more confused about economics and the financial markets. I saw a study that said half of all Americans believed that the Federal Reserve was an Indian reservation, while the other half thought it was a brand of whiskey. (Just kidding.)

But, this story is true. Last year I was giving a talk in the Midwest, and a guy came up to me at the end and told me that he enjoyed my presentation and all the jokes—but that the material didn't pertain to him personally because it was about stocks and bonds and all his money was in mutual funds. Yikes! I didn't have the heart to tell him that stocks and bonds are what generally comprise mutual funds. He seemed so happy. I guess he thought mutual funds were made of cheese!

Individual investors today are either terrified and doing nothing, making unimpressive returns by mirroring the crowd, or driving themselves to distraction through adrenalin-driven gambling on the stock market. Here's a closer look at the three generally "wallet-thinning" camps.

The Mattress Investor

These are the ones who put their money under a mattress—or let it sit in a no/low interest bank CD or money market fund, which amounts to the same thing. The folks who do this are terrified; they usually can't shut off the cable news and financial networks spewing dire economic spin. "It's bad, you know. This just in: Today, in the heartland, people began eating their young!"

Here is a good indicator. As I write this, the stock market is hitting record highs. Yet people are scared. Fear mongers blame this on an uncertain economy. Well, when the heck did we ever have a "certain economy"? It's capitalism, and capitalist economies are cyclical. It's been that way since the earth cooled.

Before you even start thinking about investing in the stock market, you need to have a few things checked on your financial to-do list. You need to pay off your credit card debt. You are paying 15 percent, 20 percent, maybe even 30 percent on those debts, and that level of return is going to be very difficult, if not impossible, to consistently earn in the stock market—even with the help of this book! In fact, paying those loans off is the equivalent of having that money earn the usurious rate you were previously paying the credit card folks.

Secondly, make sure you and your family have adequate health insurance. Far and away, the number-one cause of personal bankruptcy is the crushing burden of unpaid medical bills. Don't let that happen to you! It doesn't help to have a portfolio of exciting small-cap stocks when the bill collectors are coming to take your home and your golf clubs.

I'm not saying that individual investors should put all their money into smaller, under-followed stocks. Far from it! Your investments should be viewed as a pyramid. On the bottom, or base, are treasury bonds, CDs, high-quality corporate bonds. The middle portion of this pyramid might contain blue chip stocks (an index fund is probably best) or real estate. But on the tip of the pyramid, you have room for higher-risk, higher-return investments.

One handy measure for saving for your retirement is to subtract your age from 100: The remainder is the percent that goes into stocks. So, if you're just 30, you can take the long view on 70 percent of your portfolio, whereas if you're 75, it might not feel safe to put more than 25 percent into stocks. The reason for this is that over long periods of time, stocks have handily outperformed bonds, but stocks come with much more volatility. The longer your time horizon is, the more attractive stocks become. Generally, it's better to be an owner (stocks) than a renter (bonds).

Yes, the market has its ups and downs. Yes, the media does its level best to scare small investors into hiding with 24/7 updates from around the globe that are, I can assure you, largely irrelevant to the vast majority of companies.

But if you just let your money sit, in a bank or under your Sealy Posturepedic, its real value will decline due to inflation. Doing nothing erodes your purchasing power. Put that money to work.

The Handoff

Some investors just don't want to know. They simply hand over their money to the investment experts. This tends to lead to predictable and uninspiring results. Most of the "experts" are focusing on the same large, "picked-over" investment ideas as their counterparts.

One of the saddest, but most common, things I see is when an investor shows me his or her "diversified" portfolio of mutual funds. When you look up their skirts (OK, let's rephrase that: when you check the fund's largest holdings), you find that they all tend to own basically the same 20 or so stocks. The investor here is getting a lot of different financial documents but is not really getting much diversification.

Over the past 90 years or so, the S&P 500 has produced annualized total returns of about 10 percent. That is pretty good. Here's the bad news. For the past five years, almost 70 percent of mutual funds have underperformed their benchmarks, and the average mutual fund investor does even worse. The investment industry usually quotes "relative returns" (i.e., "You lost money BUT did better than most investors."). This is like being named "the tallest jockey."

Most investors get bullish and bearish at precisely the wrong times, in effect buying high and selling low. It seems to me that "timing the market" is an exercise in futility and usually leads to questions of your financial adviser like, "Excuse me, but what are these parentheses in my account?"

The Trader

Hunched over his or her computer screen and gulping down energy drinks, this "gambler" believes his ASD (attention surplus disorder) will allow him to capture a series of small profits.

This lifestyle has a certain Kenny Rogers appeal (...you gotta know when to hold 'em...), but in all my years of investing, I've never seen anyone consistently earn superior returns investing this way. On the other hand, they have done a great job at keeping the antacid industry solvent.

Some investors think they get an edge by quickly reacting to news. Forget it. The market receives, interprets, and factors in new information in no time! Even complicated news is quickly assessed. One of the successful companies we follow is Gulf Island Fabrication (GIFI), an oilfield marine construction company in Houma, Louisiana. The company's founder is Alden "Doc" Laborde. "Doc" is a business folk hero in this area and also created two other public companies: ODECO (since bought out by Diamond Offshore Drilling) and Tidewater (TDW), the largest owner and operator of oilfield service vessels in the world. There was even a 1953 movie about his heroics called "Thunder Bay" starring Jimmy Stewart.

S&P 500 Index vs. Gulf Island Fabrication

Range 08/29/1997	- 06/28/2013		Period Monthly	No. of Period	190 Month(s)	
Security	Currency	Price Change	Total Return	Difference	Annual Eq	
1. SPX Index	USD	78.58%	137.99%	132.30%	5.63%	
2. GIFI UW Equity	USD	-5.43%	5.69%		.35%	
3.						

Australia 61 2 9777 8600 Brazil 5511 3048 4500 Europe 44 20 7330 7500 Germany 49 69 9204 1210 Hong Kong 852 2977 6000
Japan 81 3 3201 8900   Singapore 65 6212 1000   U.S. 1 212 318 2000   Copyright 2013 Bloomberg Finance L.P.
SN 774484 EDT GMT-4:00 H444-1474-0 01-Aug-2013 17:27:34

In late 1998, Gulf Island completed a $50 million deck fabrication to be installed onto the Petronius oil platform in 2,000 feet of water about 210 miles southeast of New Orleans in the Gulf of Mexico. Petronius was a Roman satirical writer in Nero's time (and you thought those liberal arts courses were wasted). An offshore installation contractor barged the huge structure out to the rig. While workers were installing it, the cable snapped, and this valuable hunk of iron sank to the ocean floor. Every event has winners and losers. After breathing a sigh of relief that there were no fatalities, investors quickly went to work evaluating the situation. Within minutes:

- Shares of the offshore contractor fell in value (it was their error).

- The oil company's stock price remained stable (business insurance was in place).

- Gulf Island's stock went up sharply (they were going to get to build it all over again).

It's official. Wall Street is filled with quick thinkers.

A recent study by Professors Terrance Odean and Brad Barber at the University of California at Berkeley shows that those investors who trade the least outperform those who trade the most by 6.8 percent annually. I think I've always suspected this was true.

So instead, I want to show investors how to find and evaluate overlooked companies, show a little patience—and then reap the rewards by picking stocks.

You might be saying, "Hey, this guy teaches at a university. Doesn't he know that the markets are efficient and that stocks are perfectly priced based on all available information?"

The "Efficient Market Hypothesis" is an assumption that everything we are talking about here is already priced into the stock. It also assumes that what we're talking about in this book is a waste of time. There are academics wearing black socks and Birkenstock sandals walking around campuses all over America teaching that.

There are some who say that the market prices every stock at exactly what it's worth. A company's stock price is affected by many factors: projected earnings per share, strength of its balance sheet, prospects for growth, past performance, and so on. Everything is in the price. As the ads used to say about Ragu spaghetti sauce, "It's in there."

I will grant them that—but only for well-monitored companies whose fortunes attract analysts by the bushel. I'm really not having a face-off against academic finance. I'm just saying, I think academic finance is partially right. The market for blue chips is pretty darn efficient. Small companies often aren't so scrutinized. And that's where many of the opportunities lie.

Many of these gems might be right in your hometown. Or perhaps they're companies you have come across in your work, or through a friend or neighbor. In any economy, good or not, there are solid companies run by smart individuals that are going to prosper.

I wanted to show investors how to find and evaluate these overlooked companies—and then reap the rewards by investing in these stocks. Small companies are one of the best places in the market to generate "alpha"—return over and above what you'd expect to earn for the risk you have assumed by purchasing a particular stock.

Let me tell you a story about how I fell in love with the stock market. Gather 'round.

In the early 1980s, I was a young man working at Kidder Peabody & Co. investment firm in Boston (since bought out by General Electric). I lived downtown, in the North End, and every morning I would put on my suit and walk to work. The market back then opened at 10:00 a.m., and we generally had to be there by 8 a.m. But one morning, our boss told us to be in the office at 7 a.m. He wanted us to hear from an analyst who was coming in from out of town.

The stock market was flat-out awful. I remember complaining about the stock market to an older colleague. He also had money in the equally dreadful real estate market and quipped, "Yeah, but at least you don't have to paint them!" (fair enough).

Stock prices kept declining. I was ready to hear what this Wall Street guru had to say, so I got myself to work early, and...well, it was practically a religious experience for me (clouds parting, rays of brilliant light, etc.).

Just picture it. Interest rates were 18 percent, and nobody could buy a home (the interest rates made that impossible). If you had a home, you were going to stay in it because you needed to stick with your current low interest mortgage.

The analyst said, "All over America, wives are saying to their husbands, 'Honey, I know we can't move, but you are going to do something about this place. It's outdated; it looks awful. At least paint the den! If you don't, I'm moving out, and here's the best part...I'm leaving the kids with you!'"

"So," the speaker continued, "I'm recommending Sherwin Williams (SHW)." This was the Cleveland-based paint company, about as unsexy a stock as you imagine. And guess what? He was right. Homeowners did start fixing up their homes, and in less than a year, the stock was up 250 percent (four times better than the overall stock market).

That's what I mean. As they say in the South, "Every pancake's got two sides." There is no scenario that's bad for EVERYONE. In 1980, despite a challenging stock market, it was a bull market for companies that catered to do-it-yourselfers who splurged on paint to fix up their homes. No matter the scenario, somebody is going to benefit from it.

You just have to figure out who that is.

1

Hit 'Em Where They Ain't

"Wee" Willie Keeler was so good at hitting a baseball that he was inducted into the Hall of Fame in 1939. At only 5 foot 4 inches tall and 140 pounds, he credited not brawn but his brains for his success on the diamond. He said his strategy was simple: "I hit 'em where they ain't!"

In his case, "they" referred to fielders. At Tulane University's Burkenroad Reports, our student stock researchers are employing that same strategy, but the "they" we are avoiding are money managers and securities analysts.

I will grant you that some stocks are ignored for good reason. But it still amazes me how many solid and attractively priced stocks have almost nobody following them. Most people assume that companies "orphaned" by analysts have horrible balance sheets, uninspiring growth outlooks, or are so small that investors would label them "penny stocks." These characteristics would have me running the other way, too. But in many cases, they've slipped through the cracks because:

- They operate in more than one business or industry.

- They are based "out where the buses don't run," far from Wall Street.

- They don't have many shares traded on a daily basis and aren't in need of corporate finance work. They don't make very attractive clients for investment firms.

- They lack an easily identifiable "peer group." Most analysts compare relative valuations to determine a stock's attractiveness. And for this, you need a peer group of like public companies. This is similar to the way real estate agents price homes by square footage, based on the sales of comparable nearby homes.

This is an especially important concept, so let me give an example. There's a Morgan City, Louisiana, marine fabricator called Conrad Industries (CNRD). The vessels that Conrad makes are too big to compare the company to the public companies that manufacture pleasure boats, and too small to compare to those who build tankers or Navy ships. Only Burkenroad follows the stock. Such a "peerless" company often becomes an orphan stock, because analysts don't have any valuation benchmarks.

You're more likely to uncover these gems than any Wall Street professional.

Smaller companies tend to be overlooked by the big analysts, and my observation has been that the number of analysts following the stock seems to be inversely correlated to its potential performance. Apple (AAPL) has 65 analysts following it. Every time they drop a pencil, the analysts jump on it. If a horde of analysts are following a company, then the stock is probably priced efficiently and not a bargain. I look for companies where five or fewer analysts are following the stock.

Bayou Steel, a company that Burkenroad Reports followed, was profiled by *The Wall Street Journal*. They asked the CFO whether he liked having the Tulane students come over and write their reports. "Yes!" he replied. "Would we prefer to have analysts from Morgan Stanley follow us, sure, but they ain't coming!"

The point is, people far from Wall Street run across business opportunities analysts would never know about. For my money, two of the greatest investors in history are Warren Buffet of Omaha and John Templeton, who spent his time in the Bahamas. If they had been operating out of big money centers like Boston or New York, they may have suffered from "group-think" and owned the same stocks as everybody else. Be grateful for "group-think"—it leaves a lot of opportunities for the rest of us!

When I was first thinking about starting Burkenroad Reports, I went to New York and was talking to a money manager, this big, gruff guy, and I was telling him what I planned to do—going to visit and write about these public companies headquartered in the South. And he said, "Peter, that's a terrific idea. You know why?" He snorted. "Up here, they don't know anything. You know what they know? They know Starbucks! They know delicatessens!"

It was actually an important message. You're more likely to find a great company in your hometown or through the company a friend works for than the Wall Street in-crowd ever would be.

Individual investors can also have a lot more patience. Unlike professional analysts, individuals don't need to report impressive short-term results at the end of each quarter to keep their jobs. This situation always reminds me of something my investor friend Fred Speece likes to say: "Genius is just a greater aptitude for patience."

There are several reasons I think this is a great time for individuals to pick their own stocks.

The one big advantage that individual investors have nowadays is the Internet (quick, Batman, to The Google). In the past, investment information was the province of the big firms that dominated Wall Street. Investors had to depend on brokers or dig through newsletters and stock guides to figure out how much companies were worth and what their earnings potential might be. I actually remember taking a friend from another firm to lunch so that he could slip me his firm's research report on a company I was interested in.

These kinds of archaic stories, like tales of writing "order tickets" and having the order takers type them up and send them to the floor, drive my Tulane students crazy. ("How old ARE you, Professor Ricchiuti?") In truth, a lot has changed in a relatively short period of time. Working with young people is great and invigorating, but sometimes it does make you feel old. I know I'm getting old. I'm now approaching that age when the term "pulling an all-nighter" pretty much means sleeping through the night without having to get up to go to the bathroom!

And change is hard. I had a tough time getting over the stock market's 2001 move from fractions to decimal pricing. I was really good with fractions...and where can I use that skill set now? Recipes? (1/2 cup of sugar!) Racetracks? (He's coming around the 3/8ths pole!) Math is tough for a lot of people. They say that a waitress once asked Yogi Berra if he wanted his pizza cut into six or eight slices. "Six," said Yogi, "I'm not hungry enough to eat eight!"

Nowadays, investors can pull up company websites and find financial analyses, annual reports, investor slide shows, and even listen to archived conference calls. And whereas in the past, investors had to pay brokers hundreds of dollars in commission, these days ordinary people can make their own trades online for just a few dollars.

So, why aren't people taking advantage of this wealth of great information? They just aren't interested. Stock-picking is a lost art. I think it goes back to the mood of the investor. They're terrified and don't want to make a move. Or, they've been convinced that they need to let someone else manage all their investments, to go with the crowd.

Small Caps

I once noticed a solid, well-run company in Houston that made gloves, safety goggles, and other products that protected people who worked with dangerous chemicals. It was doing well, and I thought it would fit well in Burkenroad Reports. So, I called the company and got through to the CFO's secretary, and asked to speak to the guy. I told her who I was, and how we followed small public companies.

The secretary read me the riot act. She said, indignantly, "We are NOT a small company! We are a large, multinational corporation!" It was funny to me, because she was using the term differently than I was using it. The company had a market capitalization of about $700 million. That is what Wall Street calls a small-cap company, and believe me, there's nothing "belittling" about that description. Almost all of our best investments are small-cap companies!

The general public thinks of a large company as one that has a lot of employees, maybe, or has a lot of stores or big earnings. Investors, on the other hand, look strictly at what we call market capitalization. It's easy to figure: It's simply the number of shares outstanding in the company times the stock price.

For instance, a terrific, well-managed small-cap company we follow is AFC Enterprises (AFCE), better known as the fast-food chain Popeyes Chicken & Biscuits. AFC has a market capitalization of about $750 million and is currently a small-cap stock.

RPC, Inc. (RES) is an oilfield service provider we write about and has a market cap of about $3.5 billion. It is considered a mid-cap stock.

At Burkenroad Reports, we don't follow any large-cap stocks, but a good example might be Microsoft (MSFT). It has a market cap of over $235 billion and is definitely a large-cap stock...and out of our league. We also tend to avoid high-tech stocks. Plenty of investors have made money in technology stocks, but we've been successful focusing mainly on low-tech companies, and we'll continue to "dance with who brung us."

Here's a current rough gauge on market capitalization:

Large Cap = Above $10 billion

Mid Cap = $2 to $10 billion

Small Cap = $100 million to $2 billion

Micro Cap = Up to $100 million

Over long periods of time, small-cap companies have significantly outperformed their large-cap brethren. Over the last 30 years, the small cap Russell 2000 (RTY) has outperformed the large cap S&P 500 (SPX) by nearly 3-1.

S&P 500 Index vs. Russell 2000 Index

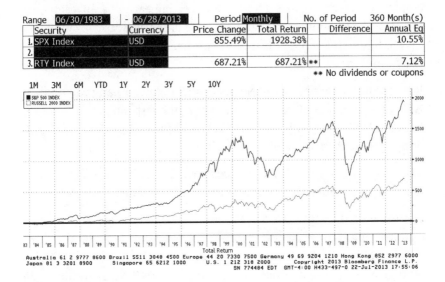

	Security	Currency	Price Change	Total Return	Difference	Annual Eq
Range	06/30/1983	- 06/28/2013	Period Monthly	No. of Period	360 Month(s)	
1.	SPX Index	USD	855.49%	1928.38%		10.55%
2.						
3.	RTY Index	USD	687.21%	687.21% **		7.12%

** No dividends or coupons

1M 3M 6M YTD 1Y 2Y 3Y 5Y 10Y

■ S&P 500 INDEX
□ RUSSELL 2000 INDEX

Total Return

Australia 61 2 9777 8600 Brazil 5511 3048 4500 Europe 44 20 7330 7500 Germany 49 69 9204 1210 Hong Kong 852 2977 6000
Japan 81 3 3201 8900   Singapore 65 6212 1000   U.S. 1 212 318 2000   Copyright 2013 Bloomberg Finance L.P.
                                                     SN 774484 EDT GMT-4:00 H433-497-0 22-Jul-2013 17:55:06

I can hear you wondering right now: If small-cap companies tend to be overlooked by Wall Street, how do investors eventually make money off them? What makes their share prices go up? Can't they just linger forever as dreaded "perma-cheaps"?

Stock Catalysts

One big reason small caps tend to beat large caps is simply based on scale. If Microsoft, which has $78 billion in annual sales, invents a new widget and sales go up by $100 million, the stock might barely register it. But if egg distributor Cal-Maine (CALM), with $1.3 billion in annual sales, picks up a new customer and grows *its* sales by $100 million, the stock would likely see a re-evaluation and a jump in its share price.

Share Buybacks

Likewise, if a company starts buying up its own shares, the amount of available stock—denominator—gets smaller A relatively small change in the fortunes of a company can have a big impact on the stock if there aren't many shares outstanding. With each share packing more worth, earnings per share gets a boost from fewer shares as well.

■

Growth Brings Attention

Although a company might be too small for Wall Street to notice right now, at some point, a successful small cap is likely to get to a size where the analysts sit up and take notice. As it gets bigger, it will get followed.

This is one of the great oddities in the world. As a company's shares get more expensive, they become more attractive to Wall Street. A company that is invisible to analysts at $10 per share and a $100 million market cap suddenly becomes an investment community darling at $100 per share with a $1 billion market cap.

The world outside of Wall Street doesn't work this way. People don't generally ignore a sweater at $10 and then fight with other shoppers at the chance to pay $100 for the same garment.

I am originally from Boston, so I saw aggressive bargain hunting first hand at the original (now bankrupt) Filene's Basement store downtown. Filene's had a system for dropping prices on items for each week they remained in the store. It was such an institution that my Dad was taught percentages Filene's style as a child in Boston's public schools (Show your work! A men's shirt arrives at Filene's Basement on March 1 and is priced at $5. The shirt's price is halved every seven days. What is its price on March 15?). I loved this place and the surly sales staff. I am color-blind and once asked a salesman the color of a particular (highly discounted) suit I had found. He answered, "What color do you want it to be?" You just don't get that kind of customer service anymore!

As a little boy, I was brought to Filene's all the time by my Mom. I will never forget watching women disrobe in the aisles to try on much sought-after items. You can imagine this made a lasting impact on me.

The Liquidity Discount

Big institutional investors need to move millions of dollars quickly in and out of a stock, and they tend to avoid companies that don't have a high number of shares outstanding, big average daily volume, or a large float of tradable shares. This lowers the valuation of "less liquid" stocks and leaves a nice opening for Mr. or Ms. Small Investor. You're in the proverbial catbird's seat. The individual investor doesn't need to be scared away by a stock's limited liquidity. You're probably not going to be buying or selling enough shares to really affect the market.

I once sent my students' research to a money manager at a big Chicago-based investment firm. He thanked me for the reports and complimented my students' work. But, when I asked him if he had purchased stock in any of these ideas, he said, "I have for my own account, but not in the fund. These stocks don't have the liquidity I need. It's tough to sell a lot of shares in these kinds of companies without knocking down the price. For institutional investors, these are called 'Hotel California' stocks. You can check in anytime you want—but you can never leave."

Because the big institutional investors shy away from these stocks, they tend to sell at more attractive valuations. We call this "the liquidity discount."

Skin in the Game

Another reason I like small caps: In many cases, a big portion of the management team's personal assets are invested in the company's stock, even though their financial planners probably say they need to be more diversified. If the stock rises, they'll be in "high cotton," but if things go south, the company managers and their families could be suddenly "downwardly mobile." I feel good when management is in the same boat as I am. Will they work hard to grow the company and get the stock price up? Is the Popemobile Catholic?

Quicker Thinking

Small caps are more flexible as economic winds shift. Managers can make decisions based on their thorough knowledge of the business and see the impact quickly—not, as with some huge companies, weeks later after layers of executives are consulted and endless meetings are held. If they need to close down a lagging product line or move personnel, it happens right away, with less costly waste.

Better Balance Sheets

Even if accounting was not your forte as a student, and all you remember from that class was that the "debits are closest to the windows," you need to think about this. Generally, smaller, unknown companies operating in seemingly "un-sexy" industries have cleaner balance sheets. There is a reason for this. They just don't have the easy access to capital as do their Silicon Valley or large-cap counterparts. This makes these managements very good "stewards of capital."

Buyout Potential

Furthermore, small caps are more likely to be bought out. Since Burkenroad Reports started in 1993, we've had 24 companies bought out. And when they do get bought out, you're more likely to have a fatter takeover premium. That is, whoever's buying the company is likely to pay quite a bit above the asking price for a small-cap company. If a big company is taken over, the premium might be 20 percent. For small companies, we've seen premiums of 50, 60, and even 100 percent.

In August 2012, one of the companies we followed, The Shaw Group (SHAW), out of Baton Rouge, was bought out by CB&I Corporation (CBI), another engineering and construction firm. Shaw was trading at $28 a share; CB&I offered $48 a share: a 72 percent premium. A few months later, New Orleans-based McMoRan Exploration (MMR) was bought out by its former parent company, Freeport McMoRan (FCX), at almost double its pre-buyout announcement price.

These small-cap "Stocks Under Rocks" aren't always in favor, and even good stocks will decline in value when the market takes a tumble. (As they say here in New Orleans, "When they raid the brothel, even the piano player goes to jail!") But, eventually human nature and economics will win out, and these kinds of stocks have a lot going for them.

2

Despicable Me

From pawn shops to pest control to convenience stores to death care, the businesses we might be embarrassed to talk about at a cocktail party can be great investments.

For instance, people like to brag about investing in companies that are developing the latest new-fangled technology. These companies are sexy and may very well change the way we live, but they're not necessarily where you want your money invested. Air travel certainly bettered the world, but airlines have been such terrible investments that Warren Buffett once quipped that "Far-sighted capitalists would have shot down Orville Wright at Kitty Hawk!"

Investors should be looking at the profitable, well-run business with a good balance sheet that is selling at an attractive valuation. Often, the stocks that are the best buys and make you the most money are in companies that won't elicit oohs, aahs, and admiration from other folks at a party.

How Much Would You Give Me for This?

Pawning is probably the world's second-oldest profession, and, with about 900 stores, Cash America International (CSH), out of Fort Worth, Texas, is the biggest and the oldest of the publicly traded pawn shops. Pawn shops might sound kind of unseemly, but the truth of the matter is, they're quite profitable and they're not going away. There are 80 million people in the United States who are without bank accounts (or, and I love this term, "unbanked"). Often, these people use pawn shops like ATMs.

S&P 500 Index vs. Cash America

Range 08/31/2012	- 06/28/2013	Period Monthly	No. of Period	10 Month(s)

Security	Currency	Price Change	Total Return	Difference	Annual Eq
1. SPX Index	USD	14.20%	16.41%		20.24%
2.					
3. CSH UN Equity	USD	17.10%	17.38%		21.45%

1M 3M 6M YTD 1Y 2Y 3Y 5Y 10Y

■ S&P 500 INDEX
☐ CASH AMERICA INTL INC

Total Return

Australia 61 2 9777 8600 Brazil 5511 3048 4500 Europe 44 20 7330 7500 Germany 49 69 9204 1210 Hong Kong 852 2977 6000
Japan 81 3 3201 8900   Singapore 65 6212 1000   U.S. 1 212 318 2000   Copyright 2013 Bloomberg Finance L.P.
SN 774484 EDT GMT-4:00 H433-497-0 22-Jul-2013 17:58:00

Let's say I have a trumpet. That used instrument might be worth $100. If I bring it to the pawn shop, I'll probably get about $50 cash for it. The pawn shop will hold my trumpet for up to 90 days. After that, it's theirs to sell.

Here's the math. If I buy it back in one month, it will cost me $60, after two months, $70, and after three months, $80. I was surprised to learn that 70 percent of all pawned items are repurchased by the owner in that 90-day window.

That is an interest rate of about 20 percent per month. For the businessman, that's fantastic. For the customer, it's a very high rate of interest, but it might be the only way they'll get a loan.

Cash America is an interesting growth story, but this growth does not come without challenges. It's a very crowded business sector. Recent high gold prices have been good for traffic, but have created many new mom-and-pop competitors. "It's incredible," one executive laughed, describing how he'd driven past a muffler shop that had a sign in front announcing "We Buy Gold." Competitors on this side of the business are "coming out of the woodwork."

Cash America was founded in 1983 by a guy named Jack Dougherty, an oil service businessman who started looking for other options when oil went bust. He chose pawning because, as he put it, "There are no dry holes in the pawn-shop business." The industry has come out of the financial shadows. There are now several pawn-shop reality shows, and a number of the stores are located in the South. My students loved shows like "Pawn Stars" and "Cajun Pawn," so we decided to investigate the category for Burkenroad Reports. (The executive we talked to said if you're going to educate yourself about their business, watch "Pawn Stars." The "Cajun Pawn" show is more like a low-end, oddball "Antique Road Show.")

Cash America has taken what used to be a small, quirky, mom-and-pop type of business and replicated its model not only nationally, but around the globe. It has grown through rapid acquisition of shops in Sweden, the United Kingdom, and Mexico. In 2006, it purchased ENOVA Financial and created an Internet-based division that does very small denomination Internet loans. Now the company is about 50 percent old-school pawn and 50 percent ENOVA. The ENOVA division might not be as well-known as its pawn-shop segment, but it sports higher profit margins and revenue growth.

They've also employed technology in a couple of other smart ways: first, by marketing pawned items on the Web, meaning far wider reach than your typical walk-in neighborhood pawn shop. If a store takes in something like a diamond-encrusted bust of Elvis (interesting, but not for everyone), they can sell it to the high bidder on eBay and not have it sitting in inventory until that special, Elvis-loving customer walks in the door. They're also trying out innovations such as equipping some stores with automated storage and conveyors such as you'd see in a dry cleaning business. This was pretty cool to see.

Each store is different. We visited a few, and it was clear that the managers were in charge, cared about what they were doing, and felt like they were helping customers. Each store has to be run by people who understand the local market and know the rules of this most heavily regulated business, which vary a great deal from state to state.

Bugs, Inc.

Another example of a profitable industry you might not be inclined to brag about at a cocktail party is pest control. It's a pretty steady business—cockroaches, termites, mice. We follow Rollins Inc. (ROL), which owns Orkin, the world's largest termite and pest control business. Their headquarters are in Atlanta. Everyone knows "The Orkin Man" but, for the most part, investors don't even know that it's a public company. The students at Burkenroad Reports are one of the few groups writing on it.

S&P 500 Index vs. Rollins Inc.

Range	12/31/2002	-	06/28/2013		Period	Monthly		No. of Period	126 Month(s)
	Security		Currency		Price Change		Total Return	Difference	Annual Eq
1.	SPX Index		USD		82.57%		127.51%		8.14%
2.									
3.	ROL UN Equity		USD		415.20%		493.86%		18.49%

Total Return

Australia 61 2 9777 8600 Brazil 5511 3048 4500 Europe 44 20 7330 7500 Germany 49 69 9204 1210 Hong Kong 852 2977 6000
Japan 81 3 3201 8900   Singapore 65 6212 1000   U.S. 1 212 318 2000   Copyright 2013 Bloomberg Finance L.P.
SN 774484 EDT   GMT-4:00 H433-497-0 22-Jul-2013 17:59:07

Louisiana's hot and humid climate makes it a mecca for bugs. When the students and I told the guys at Orkin where we were from, their eyes watered up. I could tell what they were thinking—if the whole country were as "buggy" as Louisiana, they'd be a large cap stock!

Most people know Orkin from their residential pest control business. This is profitable but also highly fragmented, with a lot of small operators out there. They also operate in the "stickier" commercial pest-control businesses, meaning they enjoy very high loyalty among clients. These customers have too much at stake to take a chance with Manny's Bug-Killing Emporium. If diners see one bug running across the restaurant floor, they don't come back.

Although the revenues for Rollins are steadily growing and predictable, they also periodically benefit from "headline scares" like those about bedbugs. Bedbugs are currently a national obsession, and they cost a lot to treat, especially in the lodging industry. (My own bug man tells me that when he travels, he keeps his luggage in the hotel bathtub to avoid possibly bringing the little critters home with him.)

When I assign companies for my students to follow, they are sometimes disappointed. They're dreading going to New York City and telling potential employers at big investment banks, "Uh, here's my report on Rollins. They kill bugs." They think they'll be laughed at. But for that guy on the other side of the desk, it's actually just the opposite. Nothing could interest him more than a profitable, growing public company he doesn't know about.

A bug-killing company sounds a tad unappetizing, so right there the individual investor is probably getting a discount on the stock. Rollins is the only "pure-play" national bug chain you can invest in. They are a very well-run and well-capitalized company. Their training program is great, particularly for the residential side. And inevitably a bunch of these people go out and start their own businesses, so Rollins is training its own competition—it's just something it has to deal with.

Rollins needs to be able to find people who look good and are trustworthy enough to walk unescorted through your house and spray for bugs, and, when it's over, go under your house and chase rats. You don't always find these characteristics in the same person. But what they have learned is that ex-military guys are very good at this.

My students love this site visit. Not only do they spend a couple of hours meeting with the company's executives, but they also get to crawl around the training facility, which is a house sliced in half so all the crawl spaces are visible, simulating the hunt for bugs and varmints.

Fully 55 percent of Rollins shares are owned by the Rollins family. While these shares are part of the company's "total outstanding shares," this stock is generally not for sale and is not included in the company's share "float." This puts off a lot of investors, but not us. As analysts, we welcome large positions held by family/management. These folks want the shares to rise as much as or more than you do.

Gas, Beer, Ice, Slim Jims, and a Lottery Ticket, Please

Convenience stores (or C-stores, as they're known in the industry) are ubiquitous. I'm on the road a lot and go to them often. But, I never thought of them as investable publicly traded companies until I came across Susser Holdings (SUSS).

Based on the Texas coast, Susser owns and runs more than 550 C-stores in Texas, Oklahoma, and New Mexico. It's a romantic story of gutsy entrepreneurship. The company started back in the Dust Bowl days of the 1930s and became a public company in 2006. The stores operate under the "Stripes" brand, so even loyal customers may never have heard of Susser, the stock.

Susser has had 24 years of same-store merchandise sales growth. That's a record most retailers could only dream about. About half of their stores have a Laredo Taco Co. store built inside. I think some of my students may be a bit reluctant to dine at a C-store, but they have all loved their Mexican-style meal on the company site visit.

S&P 500 Index vs. Susser Holdings

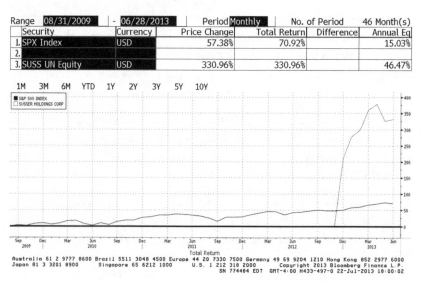

Range	08/31/2009	-	06/28/2013		Period	Monthly		No. of Period	46 Month(s)
	Security			Currency		Price Change	Total Return	Difference	Annual Eq
1.	SPX Index			USD		57.38%	70.92%		15.03%
2.									
3.	SUSS UN Equity			USD		330.96%	330.96%		46.47%

We Want to Pump You Up

When we started doing our analysis, it quickly became evident that Susser was really two businesses in one, selling gasoline outside the store and sundries inside.

Gasoline sales are usually pretty predictable and provide a solid cash flow. At most C-stores, the sales inside the store are a bit more variable with higher margins. Often, these stores see lower traffic inside when gas prices rise (as consumers feel "spent" after paying for fuel). But what many analysts don't recognize is that Susser is unique in the industry: Two-thirds of in-store customer transactions don't have fuel attached. This is at least in part because of the draw of the Laredo Taco restaurants.

To this end, Susser spun off their gasoline division into a Master Limited Partnership called Susser Petroleum (SUSP) in the fall of 2012, which provides SUSP investors with a high-yielding investment vehicle and SUSS shareholders a "pure-play" inside the store.

S&P 500 Index vs. Susser Petroleum

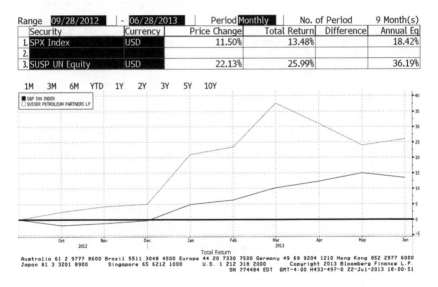

Range 09/28/2012 - 06/28/2013		Period Monthly	No. of Period	9 Month(s)
Security	Currency	Price Change	Total Return	Difference	Annual Eq
1. SPX Index	USD	11.50%	13.48%		18.42%
2.					
3. SUSP UN Equity	USD	22.13%	25.99%		36.19%

Just Dying to Meet You

Finally (no pun intended), one of the most successful companies in the New Orleans area is Stewart Enterprises* (STEI). They are the nation's second-largest owners of funeral homes and cemeteries. As someone from this industry once told me: "Business is great. People dying this year have never died before!"

S&P 500 Index vs. Stewart Enterprises

Range 08/31/1993 - 06/28/2013	Period Monthly	No. of Period 238 Month(s)				
Security	Currency	Price Change	Total Return	Difference	Annual Eq
1. SPX Index	USD	246.51%	412.19%		8.58%
2.					
3. STEI UW Equity	USD	60.29%	94.12%		3.40%

Total Return

Australia 61 2 9777 8600 Brazil 5511 3048 4500 Europe 44 20 7330 7500 Germany 49 69 9204 1210 Hong Kong 852 2977 6000
Japan 81 3 3201 8900   Singapore 65 6212 1000   U.S. 1 212 318 2000   Copyright 2013 Bloomberg Finance L.P.
SN 774484 EDT GMT-4:00 H433-497-0 22-Jul-2013 18:02:30

We followed this company for several years. It is a solid, well-run business with attractive profit margins and a predictable demand. It even makes a good play on the baby boomers. Other investors might be drawn to pharmaceutical companies or nursing homes, but I'm sticking with death care. Stewart also has a number of solid acquisition prospects with the industry consolidating. The rapid pace of consolidation of a few years back attracted the "fast money" crowd into this sector. This kind of thing changes the shareholder base to one more focused on short-term stock moves. I remember another CEO bemoaning that his company stock "used to be held by nice guys at Fidelity" and was now owned by "guys in muscle shirts!"

---

* *About the time this book went to press, Stewart Enterprises was bought out by Service Corporation, International at about a 35 percent premium (and about 50 percent higher than its average daily closing price from the previous six months).*

Mergers and acquisitions have slowed down, but organic growth is now in the mix. While touring one of their local above-ground cemeteries (that's how we do it in New Orleans, due to the high water table), one company employee joked, "I'm the last guy to let you down!" Death care humor! You can't beat it.

I think people make a mistake investing in companies they want to brag about. I've noticed that when I tell someone at a party about the stocks my students and I are following, they often respond, "I'm going to freshen my drink, I'll be right back." I never see them again. For those of us who know that less-than-glamorous stocks sometimes generate very glamorous profits, this "social shunning" is probably a good sign.

3

Investing in the Big Picture

I always like to have a few long-term themes for my stock portfolio. It pays to keep up with trends. You'll often find one or two small-cap companies that are in a unique position to benefit from the larger trends. Two that I hear a lot about are the future surge of natural gas usage (mainly replacing coal as the nation's dominant fuel source) and the reluctance of neighbors to allow chemical plants, refineries, and other industrial plants to be built in their towns. A couple of companies that have found profitable niches against this backdrop are CARBO Ceramics (CRR) and Team Inc. (TISI).

CARBO produces ceramic beads (or proppants) that improve the productivity of natural gas wells. Team Inc. sends very specialized maintenance crews to repair and upgrade the nation's rapidly aging industrial plants. You may notice that we didn't go with the more obvious choices. For instance, the natural gas boom (although "boom" isn't a welcome term in the combustible fuel industry) might suggest an investment in a natural gas driller. The geriatric industrial complex might prompt you to invest in the building of new industrial facilities.

But over time, I've learned that investors are usually better off betting on those providing services to these industries. Not many miners struck it rich during the California Gold Rush, but the folks supplying picks, shovels, and blue jeans (think Levi Strauss) did just fine.

I feel the same way about technology stocks. At Burkenroad Reports, we have never followed a true technology stock but have instead focused on the companies and industries that will benefit from these break-throughs. It always seems to me that understanding a technology business is just too tough for an individual investor. You can go to bed owning a promising stock with the latest technology and wake up with their main product obsolete because two kids invented something better in a garage somewhere.

CARBO Ceramics

Driving down Highway 61 through Cajun Louisiana several years ago (thank you, Bob Dylan), past swamps and sugar cane farms and bill-boards advertising giant seafood platters and personal injury lawyers, I stumbled on a stock tip (well, I actually found it INSIDE the car).

I was on a site visit with some of my students to one of the firms we followed, in the heart of Cajun country. Sitting next to me was a part-time MBA student who happened to be an engineer for a big energy company. His cell phone rang, and the caller was, to put it mildly, losing his mind. I could hear him yelling frantically from across the car. And my student was yelling back what sounded like "Carb it! Just carb it!"

After he hung up, I had to ask whether he'd just talked someone off a ledge. Well, no. But the caller did have an emergency on his hands. He'd been overseeing a fracturing operation, pulling natural gas through frac-tures blasted thousands of feet into the earth. The cracks were starting to close up, threatening months of work and a hefty investment.

My student was ordering his team to use CARBO Ceramics "prop-pants"—tiny, spherical, and incredibly strong ceramic beads that are slurried into the deepest cracks to prop them open, allowing oil and gas to be pumped to the surface. This is what makes fracking work.

S&P 500 Index vs. CARBO Ceramics

Range	12/31/2002	-	06/28/2013		Period	Monthly		No. of Period	126 Month(s)
	Security		Currency		Price Change	Total Return	Difference		Annual Eq
1.	SPX Index		USD		82.57%	127.51%			8.14%
2.									
3.	CRR UN Equity		USD		200.13%	236.48%			12.25%

1M 3M 6M YTD 1Y 2Y 3Y 5Y 10Y

■ S&P 500 INDEX
□ CARBO CERAMICS INC

Total Return

Australia 61 2 9777 8600 Brazil 5511 3048 4500 Europe 44 20 7330 7500 Germany 49 69 9204 1210 Hong Kong 852 2977 6000
Japan 81 3 3201 8900   Singapore 65 6212 1000   U.S. 1 212 318 2000   Copyright 2013 Bloomberg Finance L.P.
                                                  SN 774484 EDT GMT-4:00 H433-497-0 22-Jul-2013 18:03:47

When you drill a well, you're basically cracking open the earth and allowing the release of oil and gas that has been trapped down there for millions of years. To get a healthy flow, you need to "prop it open." Meanwhile, Mother Nature wants to close the opening just as soon as you've pried it open. Think about it this way. If you were in a room in which the floor and ceiling were collapsing on each other (this is basically what's happening under there), the best solution would be to fill the room full of bowling balls. This would hold the floor and ceiling apart and allow air to circulate because spheres would leave those spaces between them. This is what oilfield proppants do. They're very small (much smaller than a BB) and perfectly spherical. These innovative proppants are now essential to the oil and gas industry. At the time, they were unknown—except to a few drilling professionals.

Before long, we'd added CARBO to the Burkenroad coverage universe. Since then, the stock has climbed from $20 to nearly $180 a share. And CARBO has become a poster child for the kind of investments that have made Burkenroad successful—companies that aren't household names but are well within the reach of the smart individual investor. Then it lost almost two-thirds of its value in 2010 due to the collapse in gas prices as well as worries about the environmental impact of fracking.

Now its shares appear to be on the rise again. This is very unusual, in that investors are getting two bites at the apple here.

Our initial student visits were made to their plant in New Iberia, Louisiana—a town atop a giant salt dome (not far from the nation's Strategic Petroleum Reserve) and home of the famed Tabasco hot sauce. CARBO Ceramics is the world's largest manufacturer of ceramic proppants.

In the oilfield, the day starts really, really early. We always seem to be in a gravel parking lot on a country road by 8:00 in the morning, and we stumble out of the car to meet plant managers and workers who've probably been there since 6 a.m.

College students, of course, live on a very different schedule ("Professor Ricchiuti, I didn't know there were two 8 o'clocks!"). Once you put my students on the road, some think they are in the movie "Deliverance." We made this visit in fall, when harvested Louisiana sugar cane fields are burned to clear the stubble for the next season. We drove through the fiery countryside, past huge orange flames and billows of black smoke. Needless to say, the stacks of annual reports we'd lugged along didn't get much attention.

The proppants we had come to see start off as clay. The clay is chemically treated to form tiny spheres and fired in a cavernous kiln. Imagine a pottery class on steroids. Then they're stored in silos at the plant.

The product had taken off with the process of fracturing rock with deep explosions to let oil and gas to the surface. Fracking companies had started off using sand to prop the cracks open, but the CARBO process opened more space for oil or gas to flow. Over time, sand breaks down, the opening shrinks, and the flow of oil and gas slows. Proppants keep the fracture open longer because they are much harder: one student bit down on a few grains, curious to see how hard they were. Not a good idea, unless you wanted to visit the dentist with a cracked molar.

Sand is a competing material and has a big advantage—it's basically free. At the time, nobody was following the company, and I remember calling a couple of professional investors to ask about CARBO Ceramics. They were skeptical. "That's that stuff that competes with sand!" they said. "Good luck with that!"

It took a while for this company to gain traction. It turned out that the salesmen were talking to the wrong people. The companies that pumped the proppants into the hole didn't get it; as far as they were concerned, free sand worked fine. It just took longer to get the oil and gas out and didn't hold up as well. But the financial people at the energy companies (which actually owned these fields) quickly saw the advantages of the product's ability to deliver improved cash flow. The folks at CARBO Ceramics said they finally thought they had really made it when they were sending off barges full of proppants to Saudi Arabia!

The other question has to do with patents. Patents expire, including those on these little tiny proppants. However, the engineers at CARBO are very smart and have done a great job of tweaking the patents, constantly improving the product and its performance and making it worth the drillers' money to purchase the latest product.

What I've found is that a disproportionate number of technological advancements are adopted by small companies. It's yet another reason to focus on small stocks.

Natural gas prices have fallen recently because there's a glut, and this should mean fewer companies drilling for a while. Historically, the economics of domestic natural gas production have kept prices from free-falling. When prices dropped, rigs were laid down and supply contracted. It was a kind of "Redneck OPEC." But, shale reservoirs are huge, and turning off the pumps can do permanent damage to the field, so even when they're not economical, they keep producing, sending more supply into the equation.

There are also concerns about environmental issues with fracking. However, I think there's little chance that fracking will be banned. Because of the vast amounts of natural gas that will be available due to fracking, it's going to be a game changer: It can enable the United States to be truly energy-independent, give the country huge advantages in the cost of manufacturing, and even alter the nation's foreign policies. Unlike oil, which sells at roughly the same price around the globe, natural gas is difficult and expensive to ship abroad, and it's used, pretty much, where it's produced. Currently, natural gas prices are about twice as high in Europe and four times as high in Asia. Fracking has to be done in a responsible way, but I believe it will go forward.

Note to energy stock investors: Because of our geographic location, about 1/3 of the companies the students follow are in the energy business. But, readers should note that this industry is incredibly cyclical. Don't fall for simple statements like "we'll always need energy." The economics of this business can change overnight. I moved to Louisiana in 1983, and the energy business collapsed shortly after my arrival. It was the worst economic decline I have ever witnessed. Unemployment soared, businesses closed, and people moved away in droves. In Lafayette (the state's energy center), so many people needed to get out that moving companies were paying people to drive trucks in. My wife tells the story of when the Chamber of Commerce tried to raise spirits by putting up billboards that said "I Believe in Lafayette," and within days, the local radio DJ's started referring to those ads as "I <u>Be Leaving</u> Lafayette!"

But proving the point, the city has now come back in a big way. Today, optimism abounds and jobs go begging as the Lafayette area enjoys Louisiana's strongest economy.

Team, Inc.

Did you know there hasn't been a new refinery built in the United States since 1976? Do you know the reason? It's basically:

- NIMBY—Not In My Back Yard.
- Or BANANA—Build Absolutely Nothing Anywhere Near Anything.
- Or my favorite, NOPE—Not On Planet Earth!

As a result, industrial plants and refineries—two things that nobody wants anywhere near their neighborhood—are getting older, and as they get older, they require more maintenance and repair. Enter Team, Inc. (TISI). They've got this figured out.

A couple of trends regarding this type of maintenance: First, the chemical and oil companies would like to outsource most of it and get folks off their payrolls. They don't want to pay benefits or their salaries when they don't have to.

Secondly, they would prefer to deal with just one company nationwide. And Team is a nationwide company. At the same time, it only has 20 percent of the market—so there's plenty of room for it to grow.

S&P 500 Index vs. Team, Inc.

Range 12/29/2006	- 06/28/2013	Period Monthly	No. of Period	78 Month(s)		
Security	Currency	Price Change	Total Return	Difference	Annual Eq
1. SPX Index	USD	13.25%	30.43%	-86.91%	4.17%
2. TISI US Equity	USD	117.34%	117.34%		12.68%
3.					

1M 3M 6M YTD 1Y 2Y 3Y 5Y 10Y

Total Return
Australia 61 2 9777 8600 Brazil 5511 3048 4500 Europe 44 20 7330 7500 Germany 49 69 9204 1210 Hong Kong 852 2977 6000
Japan 81 3 3201 8900   Singapore 65 6212 1000   U.S. 1 212 318 2000   Copyright 2013 Bloomberg Finance L.P.
                          SN 774484 EST   GMT-5:00 H428-4816-0 06-Nov-2013 14:02:23

Chemical plants and refineries shut down periodically for maintenance. This provides Team with a steady and predictable stream of business. But Team is famous for hot tapping. See, if there's a leak, they can come into the facility and fix it WITHOUT shutting down the operation. That is called hot tapping (as opposed to cold tapping, when you shut down the plant to fix things), and it makes up 6 percent of Team's business.

Hot tapping is a big deal because closing down and starting up an operation can cost millions of dollars. Margins are good because these kinds of emergencies are generally not what we would call "price sensitive." You either fix it right or bad things happen. Some workers told me, "Usually, when we're arriving, there's a guy running past us down the stairs, yelling, 'It's the second door on the left...!'"

Team offers some of the best training in the country, and this type of work takes a very special kind of person. If the phone were to ring in my house in the middle of the night, I would instinctively pull the sheets over my head. But the Team experts are ready to jump out of bed and go. I personally wouldn't be good at this. It's great that there are so many different kinds of people in the world.

The company was out of Alvin, Texas (yes, the birthplace of baseball legend Nolan Ryan) and is run by a very bright guy named Philip Hawk, who spent many years with the prestigious consulting firm McKinsey & Company. It was housed in low-slung buildings in, of course, the middle of nowhere, but big things happen there because the managers are innovative and have IQs that could boil water (the headquarters have recently moved to Sugarland, Texas).

Team didn't start out doing chemical and refinery repair and maintenance. They had many misfires (they call it their 10-year walk through the financial woods). At one point, they were mowing all the interstate medians in the state of Texas. Not making much money at it, either. They stumbled initially but now have a very attractive business model.

We have been writing about Team since early 2005, but over the past few years, they've expanded both their product line and the industries it serves. Team now provides its services to several industries including aerospace, power generation, and food and beverage processing. All this requires a certain pride and confidence that is abundant in Texas.

I know this because my state, Louisiana, and Texas are neighbors and have a kind of love-hate relationship, or rivalry. The Texans are a very proud bunch, and Louisiana has this really humble Cajun culture. The old story goes that a Louisiana farmer met a Texas farmer....

> Louisiana farmer: "How big is your spread over there in Texas?"
>
> Texas farmer: "I get on my tractor and it takes me all day to ride to the end of my property line."
>
> Louisiana farmer: "Whew, I had a tractor like that once!"

See? Very different people!

4

Buybacks on the Bayou

I f you grew up in a small town, you know Teche Holdings (TSH).

My wife's family hails from Acadiana, that part of Louisiana settled by French-speaking farmers and fishermen. When we visited there, I noticed lots of billboards for Teche Federal Bank. The bank (pronounced Tesh) is named after the beautiful Bayou Teche, which runs through the region. Upon returning home, I immediately went to my computer and learned it was a publicly traded company. At the time, we were looking for companies for our student research project, Burkenroad Reports. So I called the receptionist at the bank and told her what I had in mind, thinking she'd leave the bank's CEO or CFO a message, then my people could talk to his people, and so on.

She transferred me straight to the CEO, and I had to collect my pitch in a hurry. It's that kind of place.

S&P 500 Index vs. Teche Holdings

Range 08/31/1999	- 06/28/2013	Period Monthly	No. of Period	166 Month(s)	
Security	Currency	Price Change	Total Return	Difference	Annual Eq
1. SPX Index	USD	21.65%	58.64%		3.39%
2.					
3. TSH UA Equity	USD	182.41%	344.06%		11.38%

In the fall of 1999, a group of students and I traveled to the headquarters of Teche Holding in New Iberia, Louisiana. It took a while to get there, and our second, student-driven car got two flat tires on the way. Founded in 1934, in the depths of the Great Depression, the bank was headquartered in an unassuming two-story building. The secretaries and tellers were kind, and everyone there called us "sir" or "ma'am."

Teche didn't invest in derivatives or other soon-to-be-combustible securities, and its big marketing pitch was free checking. There was a giant stack of crock pots right beside the front door. You opened a checking account, and you walked out with a crock pot.

The students were incredulous. Free checking? Giveaways? They'd heard their grandparents, maybe, talking about this kind of thing. Students at Tulane tend to be a sophisticated bunch. The students I had that year were all from New York, and a couple of them had parents who were managers at big banks, high atop massive skyscrapers. They were sort of smirking at this place way out in the country.

Thankfully, president and CEO Patrick Little and the executive team at parent company Teche Holding didn't hold that attitude against my students. These people are smarter than probably anybody these kids had ever met. But they have that genteel, Southern way about them.

They really play down their knowledge and they tend to be incredibly humble, yet it didn't take long for these kids to realize that Teche knew its business—and was making money. Lots of money.

They started talking to the students about their market—how people around there worked in agriculture, sugar, and crawfish, how many of their customers worked in the offshore oil industry. At the time, you were seeing a lot of local banks being bought out by big, national banks. The fear for the smaller banks was that they would be completely out-matched, killed off by the big guys from the big city.

As it turned out, the opposite happened. As we stood in the pleasantly quaint lobby of Teche Holding, sipping our cups of free coffee and listening to customers swap fish tales with the CEO, we saw clearly that these country people didn't want to deal with a big, impersonal city bank. Instead, as neighboring small institutions were bought up, customers moved their accounts to a place like Teche.

Nowadays, most banks seem to actively discourage people from coming into the lobby. The ATM in the parking lot is free; the lobby hours are short, and the lines inside are long. Not at Teche. They want people to come in and talk. That's how they get to know their clients, and that's how they find out who's going to expand their business and who wants to buy a new house. It's this kind of information and relationship that drives loan growth at Teche.

The checking is perfectly free to the customer, but every checking account comes with a debit card. When the debit card gets used, the bank gets a little bit from the merchant. As CEO Little said, "We have a lot of accounts, and we make a little on each one." These are graduate students, and they've learned some pretty complex formulas for calculating earnings and ratios and so on. But the CEO said, very patiently, as if he were reminding a third-grader: "Let me give you some math here. A little number ... times a big number ... is a BIG number."

Students come to Tulane from everywhere—about 75 percent of our students come from more than 500 miles away—so our trips through the rural South are real adventures for them. These students are often a bit surprised at the caliber of management they meet. They're a far cry from the characters they expect to meet because of popular TV shows like "Swamp People" and "Duck Dynasty."

Honey, We Shrunk the Float

Teche continues to grow. It has 70,000 customers and 20 offices. It's the fourth-largest publicly owned bank headquartered in Louisiana, with more than $839 million in assets. How has the stock performed? It's up about 350 percent since we started covering the company. It also pays a big and growing dividend. Increases to the dividend are not only a boon for shareholders but also signal a real confidence in the future of the company on the part of the board of directors.

Earnings per share drive the company's value, and that figure has been going up at Teche. When a company earns a profit higher than the dividend it pays out, the company's shareholder equity will rise. Over time, the market should recognize this and move the share price higher. Our students spend a lot of time trying to understand and forecast earnings. Earnings are the key factor when you're looking at a stock. Pardon my Cajun French, but the rest of it (non-earnings information) is about as significant as the buffet at a strip club. (Hey, we live in New Orleans.)

The people who are running a company—the board of directors and what is often called the C Suite, for the CEO, the CFO, and so on—know the current condition and future prospects for the company better than anyone else. And at Teche, they have the company continuously, aggressively buying back their own stock.

Teche has about 2 million shares out there (and only about 1.25 million in its float—that is, available for the public to purchase—and 750,000 shares are held by insiders). In May 2013, they announced plans to repurchase up to 3 percent—about 60,000 shares—of the company's common stock. At about $42 per share, the stock sells at slightly below its book value and pays a 3 percent dividend. Since going public in 1995, Teche has repurchased about 56 percent of its outstanding stock.

As the company buys back more of the stock, less is out there to trade in the public markets. Earnings are then divided by a smaller number of shares (in the denominator) and the all-important, earnings per share go up. Higher earnings per share (EPS) go a long way to producing a higher share price.

Critics of share buybacks argue that the move signals a lack of growth opportunities for the company. But, as you can see below, share buybacks are a very popular corporate strategy these days:

SHARE BUYBACKS OF U.S. PUBLIC COMPANIES

2009: $140 billion

2010: $299 billion

2011: $390 billion

2012: $350 billion

So, from 2009 to 2012, a staggering $1.2 trillion in stock has been bought back by companies, effectively taking those shares off the market.

Think about it. These public companies could do anything with their extra cash. They could buy Krugerrands; they could buy shares of IBM. But they know their company very well, and they decided that the best thing they could do with their money is to buy their own shares back.

When companies buy back their own stock, there are typically two reasons. One, they've got more cash than they know what to do with, and, two, they think their stock is cheap. Public companies need to do something with that cash or else run the risk of becoming the target of a leveraged buyout, and share buybacks have increasingly become the default method for spending large amounts of cash. Companies that buy back their own stock are demonstrating that they think the shares are undervalued by investors. It's like a big shout-out to Wall Street that if you won't value our company right, we're going to take our ball and go home.

These days, companies are buying back their own stocks at such a fast pace that we could have an actual shortage of stocks in seasoned, quality companies. There, I said it. If share prices don't rise to reflect what they're really worth, there will be a shortage of stocks.

Yes, new issues like Facebook have lots of shares available, but that's not the same as Teche Holdings. Teche is a dividend-paying stock with a history of operating in up and down markets. On the other hand, when a company is issuing new shares, it's a sign that the folks in charge think the stock is selling at a reasonable price (or may be over-valued).

Insider Prophets

Here we're talking about monitoring the perfectly legal insider trading that happens when company insiders buy or sell the stock for their own portfolios. They are relying on information that is available to the public. There are lots of restrictions here as to when these insiders can buy or sell shares, and these transactions require immediate public disclosure (that's how the market finds out). Watch what these people do. If they are buying the company's stock, that shows a lot of confidence. And it's a positive sign for that stock.

It's not surprising that insiders historically do much better with their buy and sell decisions than non-insiders. Here we define insiders as a company's upper management, the board of directors, and also large holders of the stock. Think of it as anyone who could easily get the CEO to answer their phone call.

The first thing to know about watching insiders is this: Insiders buying their company stock is a very bullish sign. I have yet to see a surge of insiders buying followed closely by a bankruptcy announcement. These are folks who know the inner workings of the company and its prospects better than anyone else. When they're buying shares, take notice. Googling INSIDER TRADES with the stock's TICKER SYMBOL will get you more information than you could possibly use.

On the other hand, insiders selling their shares is a less tell-tale signal. An insider buying stock does so for just one reason; he thinks the share price will rise. Insiders can have lots of reasons for selling shares. The family may be buying a home, an executive might be diversifying his holdings, tuition bills for Junior are coming in over the transom, OR they think the stock is fully or even overpriced. As an outside investor, you just don't know.

Often, you will see insiders step up to buy when a company has been very much "under-loved" by the market. As I write this, one of our Burkenroad companies, Key Energy Services (KEG), has seen a fair amount of insider buying. Its stock sells at a price significantly below its book value and the company is the leading owner and operator of workover rigs servicing the oil and gas industry. It has been a real laggard, but six insiders have purchased a total of more than 100,000 shares in the past few months.

S&P 500 Index vs. Key Energy Services

Range 12/31/2008	- 06/28/2013		Period Monthly	No. of Period	54 Month(s)
Security	Currency	Price Change	Total Return	Difference	Annual Eq
1. SPX Index	USD	77.83%	96.51%		16.22%
2.					
3. KEG UN Equity	USD	34.92%	34.92%		6.89%

Total Return
Australia 61 2 9777 8600 Brazil 5511 3048 4500 Europe 44 20 7330 7500 Germany 49 69 9204 1210 Hong Kong 852 2977 6000
Japan 81 3 3201 8900   Singapore 65 6212 1000   U.S. 1 212 318 2000   Copyright 2013 Bloomberg Finance L.P.
SN 774484 EDT GMT-4:00 H433-497-0 22-Jul-2013 18:06:43

Of course, "insider trading" is illegal, and if you do that, before you know it, you are going to be in a federal prison pumping iron and making new "friends." Insider trading involves buying or selling shares based on information that is not available to the general public. Stay away from this kind of behavior. Choose to take the moral high road. There's less traffic!

5

Contrarian Investing

To use the vernacular of country music, you're looking for "fallen angels": stocks that were once popular but "ain't loved no more." This technique targets stocks that have disappointed investors over and over until people stop paying attention.

Contrarian investors use fresh eyes to evaluate the current landscape and move beyond the past. That's where I often find real value. The nature of contrarian investing makes one a bit of an outcast. I sometimes feel like a pork chop in a synagogue.

Willbros Group (WG) is probably a good example. The stock sold in the upper $40s back in the summer of 2009 and four years later sells for only about 20 percent of that. Founded back in 1908, this is a Houston-based, world-wide company that engineers and constructs pipelines carrying oil and gas from production fields to refineries and end users. Acquisitions have broadened and diversified the company's business to include contracting for electric and natural gas distribution.

I learned about this company from my late father-in-law, who was a road contractor in South Louisiana. I was talking to him about all the challenges and obstacles that go into building a road, and one of the topics that came up was pipelines. Under the surface, Louisiana is like a plate of spaghetti, with a network of pipelines everywhere running to and from the oil patch, the refineries, and end users.

I thought this looked like the part of the industry that most investors would miss. Finding the oil and gas is the sexy part. You could hold court at a cocktail party, talking about that big oil strike. But nobody ever talks about the mid-stream part of the business, getting the product from Point A to Point B.

S&P 500 Index vs. Willbros Group

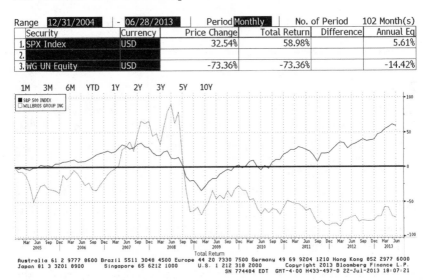

Range 12/31/2004	- 06/28/2013	Period Monthly	No. of Period	102 Month(s)	
Security	Currency	Price Change	Total Return	Difference	Annual Eq
1. SPX Index	USD	32.54%	58.98%		5.61%
2.					
3. WG UN Equity	USD	-73.36%	-73.36%		-14.42%

In doing my initial research on the company, I was intrigued by the company's use of "smart pigs" to detect cracks and blockages in pipeline systems. "Smart pigs" are electronic inspection devices that are shot through the pipelines to "squeal" on problems. I loved the name.

Willbros has had its problems. For one, they were accused of some questionable dealings in West Africa. I am not saying this is OK, but it happens to a lot of energy companies. It's frankly the Wild, Wild West over there. You want to drill? You want your crews to come back in one piece? Payoffs are often demanded in cash, alcohol, and, sometimes, a she-goat. And if you are waiting for the U.S. legal system to help you out, keep waiting.

In another tough situation, they built pipelines in Colombia and in other countries ravaged by civil wars and strife. While these contracts paid well, completions were always delayed by one chronic problem—rebels kept blowing up sections of the newly built pipelines.

The current CEO, Randy Harl, was confronted with the kidnapping of nine employees, taken from a barge operating in the Escravos River in Nigeria, in his first months on the job in 2006. After 42 tense days dealing with MEND (Movement for the Emancipation of the Niger Delta), all nine employees were safely repatriated. But operations in Nigeria were effectively ended.

After a few years of that, they'd had enough. They couldn't wait to get back to the United States, and these days, Willbros focuses exclusively on North America.

Timing is everything. New technology and new discoveries of oil and natural gas have created unprecedented momentum with the U.S. energy business. And much of this excitement is occurring in places that aren't used to having drilling crews in their communities. There are new boom towns in places like Pennsylvania, Ohio, New York, and North Dakota. We read in *The Wall Street Journal* about housing shortages, "man-camps," and strippers getting five times the rates they earned in Las Vegas!

The headlines focus on the overnight wealth of farmers and other land owners and their sometimes ostentatious spending (as a friend once described it to me, "Rolexes the size of bagels!"), but the real investment opportunity here might be in the company that figures out how to get all that energy where it needs to go. Unlike the discoveries made in traditional energy states such as Texas and Louisiana, these finds often need hundreds of miles of pipeline to get them into the grid of existing pipelines and to the refineries on the Gulf Coast. This might sound like the most mundane part of the whole enterprise, but guess what? Nothing else will work without it.

Like a shortstop in Paris, Willbros appears under-appreciated. Analysts and investors can't get past the stock's previous disappointments. But, if America is going to be energy independent, we need a way to get the oil and natural gas to the refineries and end users. Building that grid is going to keep companies like Willbros busy for decades. They could do very well. Or, a larger company could swoop in and buy them out at a nice, fat premium.

Sharps Compliance

You never know where investment inspiration will strike! This stock crossed my radar in, of all places, the men's room at an airport, where I noticed a container for the disposal of medical waste. It was marked Sharps Compliance (SMED). I suspected that diabetics are the main users of this box. Diabetes is, unfortunately, rampant in the United States, and it's widely treated by self-administered injections of insulin. These tiny, single-use needles must be disposed of, and you really don't want folks tossing them in the nearest wastepaper basket. Sharps collects medical waste in lined, trackable containers stamped for prepaid mailing and then disposes of them in its own medical waste incinerators, approved by the EPA.

S&P 500 Index vs. Sharps Compliance

Range 12/31/2009 - 06/28/2013		Period Monthly	No. of Period	42 Month(s)
Security	Currency	Price Change	Total Return	Difference	Annual Eq
1. SPX Index	USD	44.05%	55.38%		13.45%
2.					
3. SMED UR Equity	USD	-72.71%	-72.71%		-31.05%

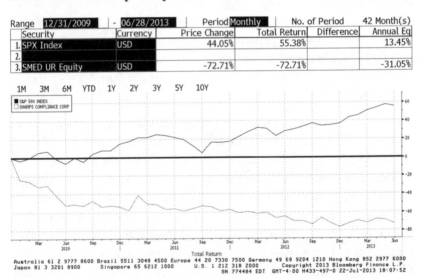

1M 3M 6M YTD 1Y 2Y 3Y 5Y 10Y

■ S&P 500 INDEX
□ SHARPS COMPLIANCE CORP

Total Return
Australia 61 2 9777 8600 Brazil 5511 3048 4500 Europe 44 20 7330 7500 Germany 49 69 9204 1210 Hong Kong 852 2977 6000
Japan 81 3 3201 8900   Singapore 65 6212 1000   U.S. 1 212 318 2000   Copyright 2013 Bloomberg Finance L.P.
                                SN 774484 EDT GMT-4:00 H433-497-0 22-Jul-2013 18:07:52

The next time I visited my doctor, there it was again—a Sharps Compliance box! I noticed how quickly the nurse took a used needle and popped it into the box. I asked her, "Where do they all go?" She looked a little baffled. "I really don't know," she said. I thought to myself, that's the best answer. For a busy doctor's office, it's important that the used needles disappear, and that you don't worry about it or give it another thought. It's no surprise that the company was founded by a doctor, Dr. Burton Kunik, in 1994.

Over the past few years, Sharps has disappointed investors, and the shares have lost close to 80 percent of their value. But this kind of unloved, nearly invisible, yet vital, business is the epitome of "Stocks Under Rocks."

If you are a hospital, you have so much medical waste that you have a company come to collect it just about every day, and of course they can't just dump it; they bring it to an incinerator.

On the other hand, if you are a smaller operation—a doctor's office, an airport where people pause to give themselves an insulin injection, or a pharmacy giving flu shots, for example—you don't really have the necessary volume to warrant a frequent pickup service, but you can't have all these needles lying around either.

So, Sharps has an effective model. It supplies customers with lined cardboard boxes for medical waste. These boxes are filled by the client, sealed, and then mailed via the U.S. Postal Service to a location in Houston that catalogues them and disposes of the waste.

It seems to me that the demand for sanitary disposal of needles is just going to get bigger. An aging population and tighter regulations on medical waste disposal bode well for this business. Did I mention that every other commercial building going up in my neighborhood these days seems to be a CVS or Walgreen's?

There is a limited number of medical waste incinerators. Sharps owns one of them. Since nobody really wants these incinerators in their neighborhood, the existing facilities have gone up dramatically in value.

While Sharps' incinerator is valued on their books at about $3 million, more recent transactions in the industry indicate that this asset could fetch many times this amount in an acquisition. This kind of mispricing isn't some asset-hiding scheme. It's the law. Under Generally Accepted Accounting Procedures (GAAP), an asset is held on the books at the lower of its cost or market price. This incinerator may very well be worth more if they were going to sell it, but their $3 million cost is what's reflected on the balance sheet. This kind of tangible valuation versus accounting valuation is often where investors can find bargains. The company has no debt, and a little more than a dollar per share in cash.

Sharps keeps coming up with markets it hasn't tapped yet. It now serves veterinarians, dentists, prisons, and assisted living facilities. It offers small, economical medical waste disposal services for individuals in their homes. One possible outcome here is that a much bigger company in the business like Waste Management (WM), Stericycle (SRCL), or some other waste disposal company may end up buying them. We'll see—this happens a lot.

6

The Beauty of Repeat Business

One of the things you should look for as an investor is predictability. It's comforting not only to have a handle on what a company's earnings are and how they make their money, but also what business might look like past the current quarter.

Just Add Water

That's why I like POOLCORP (POOL), the world's largest wholesale distributor of swimming pool supplies, equipment, and accessories. They like to boast that they sell "everything but the water." POOLCORP is one of our favorite and most successful companies, and it's headquartered in Covington, Louisiana, a quiet bedroom community outside New Orleans and not too far from Tulane.

S&P 500 Index vs. POOLCORP

Range 12/31/1996	- 06/28/2013		Period Monthly		No. of Period	198 Month(s)
Security	Currency		Price Change	Total Return	Difference	Annual Eq
1. SPX Index	USD		116.85%	194.64%		6.77%
2.						
3. POOL UW Equity	USD		2777.02%	3288.68%		23.80%

1M 3M 6M YTD 1Y 2Y 3Y 5Y 10Y

■ S&P 500 INDEX
□ POOL CORP

1997 1998 1999 2000 2001 2002 2003 2004 2005 2006 2007 2008 2009 2010 2011 2012 2013

Total Return

Australia 61 2 9777 8600 Brazil 5511 3048 4500 Europe 44 20 7330 7500 Germany 49 69 9204 1210 Hong Kong 852 2977 6000
Japan 81 3 3201 8900   Singapore 65 6212 1000   U.S. 1 212 318 2000   Copyright 2013 Bloomberg Finance L.P.
SN 774484 EDT GMT-4:00 H433-497-0 22-Jul-2013 18:08:28

The thing with swimming pools is that you have to maintain them. Otherwise they start to look like Monet's "Giverney" (that green-gooey appearance). It's estimated that the cost of maintaining an above-ground pool is $500 to $800 a year. For homeowners in the northern states, there's a chemical process when they open the pool in the summer, and another one at season's end. In the South, pools are kept filled—and the water must be treated—year round (and amazingly, here in New Orleans, the water table is so high that if you drained your pool, it would literally pop right out of the ground!).

In other words, every new pool represents a future income stream for the pool supply company, which, increasingly, is POOLCORP.

Selling the pieces and equipment to build new pools is also a big part of POOLCORP's business. And most new pools come with new houses. So when the new housing market collapsed, that particular part of the industry got whacked. Not only did the housing boom collapse, but the place where it really got clobbered was the Sunbelt, where new houses are much more likely to have pools attached to them. The pool construction market ground to a halt along with the home construction market.

But that made it clear just how attractive it is to be a two-tiered company. POOLCORP still sold chemicals and other maintenance products—that's their repeat business. All those houses up for sale in the Sunbelt? The pools need to look crystal clear for the buyers. It's not something the sellers will skimp on.

To participate in the housing recovery, you could buy shares in a home-building company. But, building new housing on spec in an economy like this—well, that is really scary. We call POOLCORP the coward's play on the housing recovery.

This stock has done phenomenally well. We started following the company in the spring semester of 1997, when the stock sold at a split-adjusted price of $1.77 per share. It traded at more than $50 per share in the spring of 2013.

I went to visit POOLCORP just before we began following it in late 1996. The CEO at the time, Rusty Sexton, got started in the pool business as a young man. When he was in college, he was dating a girl whose dad built pools. They were pretty serious, and one day her father came over to Rusty to talk to him about his future.

Cue that scene in "The Graduate" where Dustin Hoffman's character is urged to go into "plastics." The girlfriend's dad said, "The future is pools."

So Rusty said, "Do you think I should build pools?"

The dad scoffed. He said, "No, I wouldn't want any potential son-in-law digging holes in the ground. No, son, the future is distributing the equipment to build and maintain pools."

Rusty took off with this idea. He started a company called Seablue in the early 1960s and founded POOL in 1993. Now POOLCORP is the middle man between the manufacturer and the pool maintenance and construction companies—from medium-sized businesses down to what is picturesquely known as a "one-poler," the guy who pulls up in front of your house in a pickup truck with the handle of the skimmer sticking up out of the back.

Walmart, Kmart, and lots of local pool retail stores have their own lines of pool maintenance and supply products, and if you want to maintain your own pool privately, you can go to them. But if you are in the maintenance business, you go to POOLCORP.

Even in the mid-1990s, the company was dominant worldwide, and I kept spotting their facilities in places like Los Angeles, Las Vegas, and even Maine. They sold everything a pool needs. I sat down with Rusty in his office and started going through my checklist of products sold by POOLCORP.

I started off, "Do you sell kickboards?"

"Yes," he said.

"Check. Ladders?"

"Yep."

"Check. Chlorine?"

He sighed. "Peter. We have something like 35,000 products. We are going to have to step this up."

That was years ago. Now the company has more than 160,000 products in its inventory, including national brands and private labels.

POOLCORP has grown by acquiring smaller private companies. In the past, pool supply was a very fragmented business. There were hundreds of mom and pop operators. These are private companies, and you need to know one thing about buying private companies. Private companies operate their businesses to show the smallest possible profit (to keep their tax bill down), and public companies run their business to show the largest possible profit (to get their share price up). I mention this because you will often see the acquisition of a private company that looks marginal at best. But once the acquiring company goes to work on the "low-hanging fruit," like selling off the spouse's Mercedes, you get a much more positive picture.

POOLCORP has spent a fortune creating the most sophisticated distribution system in the world. And they are buying so much product that they are getting a better price than anyone else. It's all about supply chain management, and they are the masters.

Besides pool-related equipment and supplies, the company also sells accessories such as lawn furniture and built-in barbecue grills. And now that they've conquered the backyard, the company says it's coming for the front yard. It has expanded into irrigation systems, landscaping equipment, and light fixtures. The price of the stock has reflected the aggressive growth of the business. As the company slogan goes, "70 percent of the Earth is water...and we don't think that's enough."

POOLCORP's top management is an example of the kind of leaders that Burkenroad is looking for. In fact, I often check to see if top management of these successful companies serve as directors of other public companies. I learned that Rusty Sexton was a director of Houston Wire and Cable (HWCC), and we later added that company to Burkenroad Reports.

At a big company, the CEO has a certain skill set; he or she could be in charge of Caterpillar or IBM. But at the companies we follow, the executives aren't just hired hands. Their identities are very tied to the business, and they tend to own a lot of stock.

When my students last met with current POOLCORP CEO Manny Perez, they were talking about business travel. A lot of executives prefer the aisle seat so they can get off the plane more quickly. Not Manny.

"I like to sit in the window seat," he said. "I like to look down when we're taking off and landing, and look at all the pools!" He's "all in," and as an investor, you gotta love that.

I'm often asked if the successful companies we've worked with have anything in common with one another. On the surface, the answer would be no, since they are in many different businesses. But they all seem to be run by folks who are obsessively dedicated to their companies. I once appeared on the old PBS show *Wall Street Week* and stated that these managers were probably all bad golfers! And for the most part, they're hungry. These men and women worked very hard to get where they are. As is sometimes said here in the South, they weren't "born on third base and thought they'd hit a triple."

Cyberonics

Here's another kind of repeat business that investors should be aware of: medical needs.

If you have epilepsy, there are about a million drugs doctors can try on you. And keep trying. But if none of them works, the insurance companies let you get a device that is implanted near your collarbone with a very tiny metal lead that goes up to your brain. This procedure, called vagus nerve stimulation (VNS), is very advanced, and very costly, but also can be very effective.

Cyberonics (CYBX) is the company that manufactures this gadget, which made its clinical debut in 1988. I learned about this company through its CFO, Greg Browne. I'm a director of a publicly traded home health company called Amedisys, and Greg was our CFO for many years. After Hurricane Katrina, Greg moved to Houston to take a job with Cyberonics. Greg is a guy who has taken companies and turned them around. He's just the kind of CFO who really understands Wall Street and finds a way to explain a company's story to analysts. He approached Burkenroad to see if we would follow Cyberonics while there was "still some hair on the story," as he put it—in other words, before it had made all the needed changes. I'm sure glad he called.

S&P 500 Index vs. Cyberonics

Range 12/31/1996 - 06/28/2013	Period Monthly	No. of Period	198 Month(s)			
Security	Currency	Price Change	Total Return	Difference	Annual Eq
1. SPX Index	USD	116.85%	194.64%		6.77%
2.					
3. CYBX UW Equity	USD	1384.57%	1384.57%		17.76%

Total Return
Australia 61 2 9777 8600 Brazil 5511 3048 4500 Europe 44 20 7330 7500 Germany 49 69 9204 1210 Hong Kong 852 2977 6000
Japan 81 3 3201 8900   Singapore 65 6212 1000   U.S. 1 212 318 2000   Copyright 2013 Bloomberg Finance L.P.
SN 774484 EDT   GMT-4:00 H433-497-0 22-Jul-2013 18:09:24

As it happens, VNS therapy is good for more than treating epilepsy. It can also be effective in dealing with depression that resists other treatment. And of course, the depression market is many times larger than the size of the epilepsy market. Cyberonics was trying to go after the depression market, but meeting a lot of headwinds. When I asked whether the company was working on a test to prove that the device worked for depression, they told me they knew it worked. They were just trying to get insurance companies to pay for it.

And there's the rub. You can have a fabulous medical device, but if insurance won't pay for it, you don't have much of a business. Management decided that the company needed to refocus its vision on its core market, epilepsy, for which it is not only approved by insurance, but has a potential worldwide market. More and more doctors are learning about this effective procedure every year, and so far, more than 60,000 patients have used VNS therapy for the treatment of refractory epilepsy.

When we visited Cyberonics, we learned that there was an amazing underlying story that was really the key to growing earnings. The device is implanted, but periodically the product and its batteries need to be replaced. So, every time you add one of these epilepsy treatment devices to the base, it adds to the future stream of revenue.

It's similar to pacemakers, except that the VNS device is often implanted into patients at a very young age. It will be needed for decades.

The stock has performed very well. It has about tripled in price since we began covering the company at about $18.50 in the fall semester of 2008. Repeat business is a great story in a stock.

7

Niche Opportunities: Seeing What Others Missed

A few years ago, I was at my mother-in-law's fishing camp on Three Mile Lake in Southwest Louisiana, and as I was walking around with my fishing pole, I noticed a crew of guys building a pipeline. So, of course, I went over and asked what it was for—oil or gas?

They laughed and said neither—it was for CO_2. The crew was building a pipeline to transport good old carbon dioxide into old, supposedly tapped-out oil fields not far away. This is kind of like shooting Coca-Cola under the field to recreate the pressure needed to get the remaining oil up to the surface. This is an operation called tertiary oil recovery.

That's how I got to know Denbury Resources (DNR), a company out of Dallas that brings new life to old "dead" oil fields. They have developed a sophisticated network to gather CO_2 and get it to where it's needed. The ticker symbol of DNR is unfortunate, as these initials also stand for "Do Not Resuscitate" in the healthcare field. I was once interviewed by Barron's writer Christopher Williams about the company, and it was emphasized that despite this, Denbury Resources "was a keeper" for energy investors!

S&P 500 Index vs. Denbury Resources

Range 08/31/2009 - 06/28/2013	Period Monthly	No. of Period 46 Month(s)			
Security	Currency	Price Change	Total Return	Difference	Annual Eq
1. SPX Index	USD	57.38%	70.92%		15.03%
2.					
3. DNR UN Equity	USD	13.80%	13.80%		3.43%

1M 3M 6M YTD 1Y 2Y 3Y 5Y 10Y

■ S&P 500 INDEX
□ DENBURY RESOURCES INC

Sep 2009 · Dec · Mar · Jun 2010 · Sep · Dec · Mar · Jun 2011 · Sep · Dec · Mar · Jun 2012 · Sep · Dec · Mar 2013 · Jun

Total Return

Australia 61 2 9777 8600 Brazil 5511 3048 4500 Europe 44 20 7330 7500 Germany 49 69 9204 1210 Hong Kong 852 2977 6000
Japan 81 3 3201 8900   Singapore 65 6212 1000   U.S. 1 212 318 2000   Copyright 2013 Bloomberg Finance L.P.
                                                          SN 774484 EDT GMT-4:00 H433-497-0 22-Jul-2013 18:09:59

When you drill an oil well, about 50 percent of the oil gushes, flows, and then eventually seeps to the top under its own pressure. But at some point, the well loses its "oomph," and you don't have the necessary pressure to get the remaining oil. This lost pressure is why you see those iconic pump jacks that bob up and down to pump out more oil—what the industry calls "artificial lift."

Another form of artificial lift is to pump CO^2 into these so-called "mature" oil fields. This added "oomph" is sometimes jokingly called the Viagra of the oil patch. Denbury traces its past back to 1951, but its current structure began when they purchased the Heidelberg field in Mississippi from Chevron in 1997.

The fields around my fishing hole had been drilled in the 1950s or '60s. Landowners hadn't received a royalty check out of them for years. Geologists with Denbury can determine which fields will respond well to the CO^2 technology. But the tough part is to get the CO^2 to the oil field, and Denbury has built an extensive pipeline network to do just that.

The CO^2 comes from a couple of sources. First, it occurs naturally in the thick salt layer beneath our feet in Louisiana and Mississippi. But brilliantly, Denbury also goes to chemical and industrial plants, which produce CO^2 as a waste and need to account for it under federal greenhouse gas emission laws. Those plants are only too happy to supply

Denbury their CO^2, and it is put to good use in the oil fields. Basically, Denbury delivers the CO^2 and drills the field. You know what they say: "One man's trash...."

Evolution Petroleum

Sometimes when you find a great concept like tertiary recovery, it's worth looking into other players in the space. As the websites helpfully suggest in online shopping, "Those who enjoyed this product also purchased...." In this case, it was Denbury management that opened our eyes to Houston-based Evolution Petroleum (EPM), which is partner in some recovery projects with Denbury. Like Denbury, Evolution focuses on tertiary recovery and bringing old fields back to life, but Evolution is much smaller. Founded in 2003, Evolution had another feature Burkenroad likes to see in a stock, in that its employees own about 21 percent of the outstanding shares.

S&P 500 Index vs. Evolution Petroleum

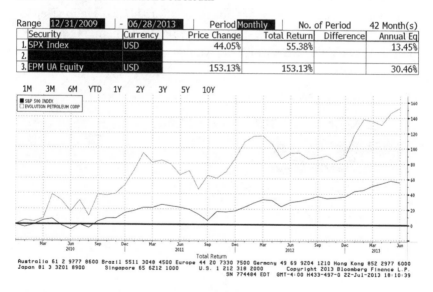

Range 12/31/2009	- 06/28/2013	Period Monthly	No. of Period	42 Month(s)
Security	Currency	Price Change	Total Return	Difference	Annual Eq
1. SPX Index	USD	44.05%	55.38%		13.45%
2.					
3. EPM UA Equity	USD	153.13%	153.13%		30.46%

Evolution kind of hit the mother lode when it bought the legendary Delhi oil field in Northeast Louisiana. This was a big, monster discovery back in the 1940s. Having produced 190 million barrels of oil since it was first discovered, the field was producing less than 20 barrels per day when EPM purchased it.

By putting it in play for tertiary CO^2 redevelopment with Denbury as the operating partner, independent geologists believe it may possibly produce another 66 million barrels, and likely still not be fully depleted.

The hope is here that these forgotten former "star oil fields" are brought back to life. This is much like old celebrities who seem to always come back to life in casinos and places like Branson, Missouri. Hello, Yakov Smirnoff!

Amerisafe

Another uber-successful niche player is Amerisafe (AMSF). Based in the bustling metropolis of DeRidder, Louisiana, this company provides workers' compensation insurance to employers that, frankly, most insurance companies want to avoid. Amerisafe focuses on small to mid-sized employers who hire roughnecks, roustabouts,. and lumberjacks. The company has grown and now serves customers in 35 states and the District of Columbia. I'm infamous for the vague driving instructions I give to my students. As they set out on the four-hour drive for DeRidder, on the Texas-Louisiana state line, I might tell them, "If you see a sign that says 'ENTERING TEXAS,' you've gone too far!"

S&P 500 Index vs. Amerisafe

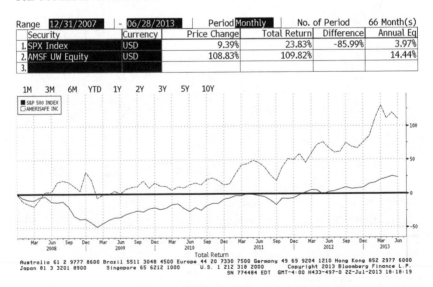

Range	12/31/2007	-	06/28/2013		Period	Monthly		No. of Period	66 Month(s)
	Security		Currency		Price Change	Total Return	Difference		Annual Eq
1.	SPX Index		USD		9.39%	23.83%	-85.99%		3.97%
2.	AMSF UW Equity		USD		108.83%	109.82%			14.44%
3.									

Here's the thing. Amerisafe understands the risks in the businesses they insure better than most everybody else, including the big insurance companies. For instance, management once asked my students if, for the same insurance premium, they would rather insure a truck carrying milk or a truck hauling gasoline. The unanimous response was the milk tanker because of, well...the "kaboom" factor. As it turns out, taking highway exits is the most dangerous maneuver for truck drivers, and milk tankers are far more likely than gasoline trucks to have an accident. This is because milk is usually held in a single tank container (the sloshing weight-transfer is the culprit), whereas, due to its flammability, gasoline tankers are divided into multiple sections. I would not have thought of that. But they did.

We have seen so many examples of successful smaller companies seizing a misunderstood market. One year, I had a student who questioned their focus on "low-frequency, high-severity accidents" (I love that term) and suggested diversifying into lower-risk markets such as assembly plants. An executive with the company laughed and told her that those jobs are lousy with carpal-tunnel claims...and they're contagious!

8

Lessons Learned

"If we knew what we were doing, we wouldn't call it research"
—Albert Einstein

In the stock-picking business, they say that if you are right 60 percent of the time, you're a big success. It's not like shooting free throws in the NBA, where if you hit only 60 percent, you'd be selling popcorn in the stands. In the stock-picking business, 60 percent is not a bad percentage.

I often tell people, when you meet a new money manager or financial planner, be wary if he or she doesn't come forth early on with the mistakes they've made. I've had some real lollapaloozas. The first one came when I was 23 years old and working for Kidder Peabody & Co. in Boston. I would hope that I've learned some things since then, but maybe not.

The firm's research department had a stock idea...and it turned into a big loser. The company was called Minnetonka, and it made soft soap. What a perfect product! No more bathtub slips on a bar of soap. The company later came up with a related product called "Toothpaste on Tap." Another much-needed breakthrough, or so I believed. Think of all the marriages that could be saved by eliminating the arguments about how the tube is squeezed and who didn't put the cap back on the toothpaste. The products sold like hotcakes.

At that time, I was building my client base. To expand my horizons and meet more people, I decided that I needed to speak at all the Kiwanis, Rotary, and Lions clubs in my sales area. Heck, I'd take a gig at a birthday party or bar mitzvah if it were offered. I had a little red Jeep, and I drove it all over New England. I must have given 200 speeches, usually lunch or dinner talks. I ate a lot of chicken.

(I really try to spice up my speeches with jokes and anecdotes. Economics and finance can get pretty dry. I was once listening to a panel of three economists and kept thinking, why does the government bother with water-boarding?)

In retrospect, this was not the most efficient way to build a business, but it taught me what I really love—I love to speak. I started keeping a diary of ideas and jokes that made people laugh. I now give about 60 speeches a year and work with more than a dozen speaking bureaus. People wanted to hear stock ideas, so I told them about Minnetonka. I had this stock in a number of client portfolios. And then one day, an article came out in *Forbes* magazine about the flagship soft soap product, asserting that "any fool with an oar and a bucket could make that stuff." I'll never forget that sentence. They were right, of course. Then another company got into the business, a little company in Cincinnati. What was their name? Oh yes, Procter and Gamble! The stock began heading south.

The stock was falling, but I was in denial. I loved that stock! Even though there were cheaper alternatives, I thought people might stay loyal to Minnetonka's product line. Didn't some people actually decorate their bathrooms around the product's look?

But the stock just kept dropping. The company was eventually bought out by a giant cosmetics company, but at a level much lower than the prices at which I bought the shares.

You should never fall in love with a stock. Love the man or woman in your life, or even your dog. But don't fall in love with a stock. You'll lose the objectivity it takes to determine when you and your investment need to part ways. You need to be able to say—even to your stock—"It's not you, it's me."

Although this was long before Burkenroad, this is a lesson and a story I brought into the classroom. I learned an important (and expensive) lesson about stock selection. When facts are coming at you, you have to take notice. The market doesn't care what you paid for the stock. No matter how painful, no matter what your cost basis is, when faced with new information, you have to take it into account. In the end, economics and truth always win out.

Piccadilly Cafeterias

Another example of investing mis-adventure would be Piccadilly Cafeterias, a company we wrote about for quite a while at Burkenroad Reports. It so happened that the years we followed Piccadilly, my children were under 10 years old, so not only did we follow them, I ate there a lot. Piccadilly is an institution in a lot of towns in the South, and certainly in New Orleans. I used to laugh because in New Orleans, you know you have it made when you have your own waiter at a high-end restaurant like Antoine's or Galatoire's. When my sons were little, we had our own waitress at Piccadilly. Her name was Miss Annie, and whenever we came in, she would carry the boys' trays to the tables for them.

I went to a cafeteria near Tulane one day with the students. On our way, one of the young coeds on the Piccadilly team told us how excited she was to be going back there. "I became a woman at Piccadilly," she declared. I almost drove the car off the road. I finally couldn't take it anymore, and I asked her, "What did you mean by that?" She said, kind of nostalgically, "I remember the first time they let me carry my own tray."

Piccadilly is a good example of how some concepts don't travel well. In the South, cafeterias are very viable places to eat. Elsewhere they are not, so Piccadilly could not successfully expand beyond its defined footprint. The company tried to open cafeterias in cities like Chicago, and it didn't work. They are not part of the tradition up there. Outside the South, cafeterias just remind people of terrible times in their lives, like hospitalization and middle school.

The restaurants are filled with the really young and really old. The average customer's age is probably 40, but there aren't really any 40-year-olds in there. There were lots of 5-year-olds and lots of 75-year-olds. Hmm, what a great way to teach the difference between the mathematical terms of average and median!

Piccadilly was one of those companies that my students are not initially excited about following. But after they began to understand the business model and its drivers, they were mesmerized. Once we were going through the line and the CFO was in front of me, and he was kind of looking up in a pensive way, and I asked him what he was thinking about. He said, "You know, Peter, if about half the people who get water at the end of the line got iced tea instead, we could add a couple of additional cents to our earnings per share." These students had been building financial models on Piccadilly, and their eyes lit up at this statement. This is a complicated and variable business, way more involved than just fried okra and middle-aged women dishing up gumbo.

I was meeting with the Piccadilly CFO and I asked him whether there were any hidden assets. "Nothing I can put a dollar figure on," he drawled, "but about half the preachers in town, when they're winding up their sermons, they say, 'Now, I know we all want to get to Piccadilly....' How much is that worth?"

But Piccadilly was eventually sunk by two events. First, they took on debt to buy the Morrison's Cafeteria chain in 1998 and then changed the name of those stores to Piccadilly. This not only put financial strain on the company, but some loyal Morrison's customers balked at the new name. You and I, truthfully, couldn't tell the difference between the menus if someone put a gun to our heads. But the customers at cafeterias tend to be, how should I put this, a bit long in the tooth. Old people generally don't like change, and many Morrison's customers stopped going to restaurants where they'd eaten for the past 40 years.

But what finally killed Piccadilly's stock was the company's defined benefits pension plan. When the stock market declined in 2000, the plan went from overfunded to underfunded and this (together with the increased leverage from the Morrison's acquisition) broke the company's back. In a defined benefits plan, the employees put in a defined amount and the company guarantees them a retirement income stream for the rest of their lives. Now, of course, most companies have gone to IRAs and 401(k)s. They take the investment risk away from the employer and onto the employee. Additionally, they're portable, they are a great vehicle for building up wealth, and they allow you to leave something for the next generation.

The benefits plan gave me a case of the heebie jeebies, because I had been the chief investment officer with the state of Louisiana and the state had an underfunded defined benefits plan—a huge financial obligation and not enough money to pay for it. I'd seen the havoc this could cause. There are some very serious rules about pension plans, and a slowdown in business doesn't allow you to slow down your payments to the plan. This unfunded accrued liability eventually spelled the end for Piccadilly. The stores still operate but under a different, private ownership.

Piccadilly is a company that has always had a special place in the hearts of customers. Every spring, Burkenroad holds an investment conference. Ours is the only one that's completely open to the public. All the others are open to professionals only. I remember when the Piccadilly CFO came to speak. The first person who stepped up to the mic asked about operations and earnings. The second question came from a bedizened older woman who asked why they didn't have the carrot soufflé any more at the Jefferson Highway store.

Piccadilly Cafeterias struggled mightily, was bought by the Yucaipa Companies in 2003, and has been operating under bankruptcy since 2012. Sure, I loved Piccadilly. But you can't be romantically involved with your stocks. You have to look at the numbers and face the facts. Oh, and definitely find out whether they have a defined benefits plan.

9

The Best Company You've Never Heard Of

G ood stock ideas can come from an unlimited number of sources, and I would much rather get a stock idea from Main Street than Wall Street.

About a dozen years ago, I had a student whose family friend operated an oilfield service company, and thought it might make a good company for Burkenroad to follow. The student made the connection, and the CEO was very impressed by our methods of finding and researching solid, lesser-known stocks.

The CEO turned out to be Charles Fabrikant, founder and largest individual shareholder of SEACOR Holdings (CKH), then called SEACOR SMIT. When I called the company, they agreed to meet with me and my students. Although the company is somewhat famous for not spending much time with analysts, it turned out that Mr. Fabrikant really had a place in his heart for education. All of a sudden, we found ourselves as one of the only groups following this great company.

S&P 500 Index vs. SEACOR Holdings

	Range 12/31/2001 - 06/28/2013	Period Monthly	No. of Period	138 Month(s)		
	Security	Currency	Price Change	Total Return	Difference	Annual Eq
1.	SPX Index	USD	39.91%	77.25%	-103.48%	5.10%
2.	CKH UN Equity	USD	130.70%	180.73%		9.39%
3.						

1M 3M 6M YTD 1Y 2Y 3Y 5Y 10Y

■ S&P 500 INDEX
□ SEACOR HOLDINGS INC

2002 2003 2004 2005 2006 2007 2008 2009 2010 2011 2012 2013
Total Return

Australia 61 2 9777 8600 Brazil 5511 3048 4500 Europe 44 20 7330 7500 Germany 49 69 9204 1210 Hong Kong 852 2977 6000
Japan 81 3 3201 8900   Singapore 65 6212 1000   U.S. 1 212 318 2000   Copyright 2013 Bloomberg Finance L.P.
SN 774484 EDT GMT-4:00 H433-497-0 22-Jul-2013 18:19:37

Why is it under-followed? SEACOR just didn't schmooze Wall Street. Management didn't offer earnings guidance; it didn't even have conference calls. They thought their time would be better spent running the company (and I think they're right). We had stumbled upon one of the most shy, hidden, and impressive public companies in America.

SEACOR is an oilfield service boat company—mostly. But Fabrikant is also a very smart and opportunistic investor with a keen sense of value and has owned fleets of helicopters, river barges, trading companies, and more. The company operates in very cyclical businesses and has skillfully bought assets when they're cheap and sold them when they're dear.

All this movement makes it tough to forecast earnings and is one reason the stock lacks the analyst coverage of its competitors, such as Tidewater (TDW) and Hornbeck Offshore (HOS). It's not considered a "pure play." This diversification, however, has paid off handsomely when one of their business sectors hits a rough patch. For instance, drilling activity in the Gulf of Mexico goes through boom and bust swings. When it's down and really quiet, the Gulf of Mexico has been referred to as "the Dead Sea" by oil field analysts. The boats that service those wells are moored in places like Port Fouchon, Louisiana, or Port Arthur, Texas— out there idle, "just choking a post!" It's times like these that investors value SEACOR's diversification and business acumen.

Generally, a well-managed, successful company will see an increase in its book value. There are several ways to measure this growth, but the best (for my money) is CAGR (Compound Annual Growth Rate). You may want to think of CAGR as a way to "smooth out" a growth rate. SEACOR's CAGR is very impressive. In fact, over the past 20 years it has not only handily beat the S&P 500 but also has nearly matched the book value growth rate of Warren Buffett's Berkshire Hathaway (BRK). This is pretty much the gold standard of the investing world.

BOOK VALUE CAGR (1992–2012)

S&P 500	+6.9%
SEACOR Holdings	+12.1%
Berkshire Hathaway	+13.6%

What you see on financial statements is the accounting book value. Ideally, investors want to find the company's tangible book value. In reality, a company can be worth more or less than its accounting book value. What tends to be understated on the balance sheet are appreciated real estate and assets that don't depreciate as fast as the tax laws say. On the other hand, companies holding inventories of outdated technology or even perishable items (think rotting tomatoes) can have a book value that is overstated. Another item that appears in accounting book value that is subtracted from tangible book value is goodwill. Tangible book value measures the current value of the company's assets. In other words, how much would you get if you were to sell these assets today?

Price-to-Book Value

This measurement is definitely more helpful in evaluating some industries than others. For instance, technology companies are more likely to have their value in patents and intellectual property than in equipment and bricks and mortar, and the price-to-book value doesn't capture this.

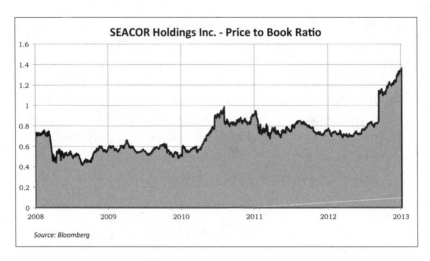

SEACOR Holdings Inc. - Price to Book Ratio

Source: Bloomberg

A graph like this can provide some perspective on a company's historic valuation. SEACOR's stock has traded in a valuation range of 67 percent of its book value up to 133 percent of its book value.

If you find a company where the book value is higher than the share price, well, that's at least an eye-opener. It means that management could sell off the buildings and equipment, pay off the debt, and generate more dollars per share than the current stock price. Sometimes investors say that a company like this is "worth more dead than alive."

In late 2012, SEACOR announced plans to spin off its Era helicopter business. This should certainly simplify the company in the minds of analysts. Spin-offs can also create great investment opportunities. (See our earlier discussion of Susser Petroleum, MLP.) I've been in the investment batter's box now for almost 35 years, and it seems that the stock of the spun-off company usually outperforms the parent company stock. Like so much of investing, this seems a bit counterintuitive. Shouldn't the parent company be shedding the portions of the business with the least potential? Well, maybe, but I find that these divisions were often treated as stepchildren within the corporate structure and are now run by the people who know this business best. The separately traded stock provided a currency to reward management's accomplishments.

S&P 500 Index vs. Era Group

Range 01/22/2013	- 06/28/2013	Period Daily	No. of Period	157 Day(s)
Security	Currency	Price Change	Total Return	Difference	Annual Eq
1. SPX Index	USD	7.62%	8.68%	-31.23%	21.35%
2. ERA UN Equity	USD	39.91%	39.91%		118.33%
3.					

1M   3M   6M   YTD   1Y   2Y   3Y   5Y   10Y

■ S&P 500 INDEX
☐ ERA GROUP INC

Jan 31   Feb 14   Feb 28   Mar 15   Mar 29   Apr 15   Apr 30   May 15   May 31   Jun 14   Jun 28
2013
Total Return

Australia 61 2 9777 8600 Brazil 5511 3048 4500 Europe 44 20 7330 7500 Germany 49 69 9204 1210 Hong Kong 852 2977 6000
Japan 81 3 3201 8900   Singapore 65 6212 1000   U.S. 1 212 318 2000   Copyright 2013 Bloomberg Finance L.P.
SN 774484 EDT   GMT-4:00 H433-497-0 22-Jul-2013 18:23:40

Frugal Is Fantastic

The reason for these strong results is that SEACOR runs a really tight ship (pun, moan). I like the idea of being frugal. At some companies, the egos and overall hubris take over. I frankly hate to see a shiny big building with the company's name on it, and I'm always taken aback when I visit a company and they've got expensive art on the walls. The lavishness is almost always for the benefit of the executives, not shareholders.

Once in the mid-90s, we went down to Morgan City, Louisiana, for the christening of a new SEACOR crew boat. It was a very fast vessel for bringing oilfield personnel out to the deep water drilling locations (once your crew leaves the pier, they're on the clock—so the faster the boat, the better).

It was a beautiful, sunny day and there was a big tent, with lots of food, and there were hundreds of people there. Miss St. Mary Parish was in attendance, in her tiara and sash. The boat was decorated with balloons and flowers, and there was a big cake in the shape of the vessel that was five feet long!

It happened that they were naming the boat after the president of SEA-COR Marine, Milt Rose, but it was a surprise to him—he didn't realize it until he went to the ship's bow (with christening bottle in hand) and saw his wife and daughters walking up the gangplank.

It was a great party. Then all of a sudden, a group of guys marched up to the boat, took down all the balloons, and folded up the tables. We're still standing there on the bank eating our cake when the boat revved its engines and sailed out of the dock. It was headed for Brazil. The party was over. That boat needed to go make money!

This was not surprising to me. I'd always heard that SEACOR began by acquiring a company named NICOR. They called themselves SEACOR to save paint as they re-marked the ships!

Other Great Penny-Pinchers

Burkenroad follows other great companies that are also set apart by their frugality. Because its strategy is to locate next to Super Wal-Mart locations in small communities, Hibbett Sporting Goods (HIBB) doesn't need to spend a lot on advertising. When I asked management about attracting customers, a company executive told me, "Listen, all I care about is that you can see us from the Wal-Mart parking lot." Hibbett keeps all its stores a couple of degrees warmer than everyone else in the summer, and cooler in the winter, and has saved oodles of money. You multiply that savings by 800 stores (in small to mid-sized markets), and it's an enormous amount of money.

The stores themselves are only about 5,000 square feet (versus the 50,000–60,000 square foot "boxes" most of their competitors operate). These smaller stores provide lower overheard and also make it less costly to close un-economic stores. Most of the merchandise coming into a Hibbett store comes in cardboard boxes. Unlike most other companies, they don't just cut open and throw away the boxes. They open them on the seams, and they reuse the boxes. When a company is vigilant and can keep costs down, that's a long-term benefit that you can feel good about as an investor.

The graph below shows that Wall Street agrees.

S&P 500 Index vs. Hibbett Sports

Range	08/30/2002	-	06/28/2013		Period	Monthly		No. of Period	130 Month(s)
	Security		Currency		Price Change	Total Return	Difference		Annual Eq
1.	SPX Index		USD		75.34%	119.89%	-603.46%		7.54%
2.	HIBB UW Equity		USD		723.35%	723.35%			21.48%
3.									

```
1M   3M   6M   YTD   1Y   2Y   3Y   5Y   10Y

■ S&P 500 INDEX
□ HIBBETT SPORTS INC
```

Australia 61 2 9777 8600 Brazil 5511 3048 4500 Europe 44 20 7330 7500 Germany 49 69 9204 1210 Hong Kong 852 2977 6000
Japan 81 3 3201 8900   Singapore 65 6212 1000   U.S. 1 212 318 2000   Copyright 2013 Bloomberg Finance L.P.
SN 774484 EDT GMT-4:00 H433-497-0 22-Jul-2013 18:25:11

More welcome frugality: Conn's (CONN) is an electronics and furniture retailer that generates a sizable portion of its earnings through its credit operations. About 90 percent of its business is done on credit, and about three-quarters of that business utilizes Conn's own credit division. Several years ago, we went to meet Conn's management at their headquarters in Beaumont, Texas. It was after one of those mid-level hurricanes. Their corporate headquarters was an old Kmart. They'd draped a new Conn's sign over the Kmart sign, and the storm had knocked off a part of it, so the K was showing. You gotta be happy with that kind of frugality.

S&P 500 Index vs. Conn's Inc.

Range	12/30/2005	-	06/28/2013	Period	Monthly	No. of Period	90 Month(s)
	Security		Currency	Price Change	Total Return	Difference	Annual Eq
1.	SPX Index		USD	28.68%	51.51%	-4.07%	5.70%
2.	CONN UW Equity		USD	55.58%	55.58%		6.07%
3.							

Total Return

Australia 61 2 9777 8600 Brazil 5511 3048 4500 Europe 44 20 7330 7500 Germany 49 69 9204 1210 Hong Kong 852 2977 6000
Japan 81 3 3201 8900   Singapore 65 6212 1000   U.S. 1 212 318 2000   Copyright 2013 Bloomberg Finance L.P.
SN 774484 EDT GMT-4:00 H433-497-0 22-Jul-2013 18:25:56

I'm reminded of another example of smart management at Conn's. Back in the early 2000s, big, flat-screen TVs were all the rage, and Conn's had a great selection. Back then, Conn's didn't sell furniture but realized that customers could get the whole feel of the "at home" big screen experience if they could watch the sets sitting in a recliner. So, they found a recliner manufacturer and asked them to ship chairs to them as "props" (not actually for sale). Well, Conn's didn't really care much what they looked like, they just wanted a good price, and in came dozens of gaudy silver and blue recliners. Customers liked the TVs but *loved* the chairs! See, this is Texas, and silver and blue are the colors of the Dallas Cowboys. Management quickly began selling them, ordered more, and today they are really big players in furniture retailing too!

Throughout this book, you'll see that many of the best companies keep their costs down by setting up their operations outside of expensive metropolises. We find terrific companies in small, often poor, communities. As Louisiana political consultant James Carville once said, "Some of these little towns are so poor that the local high school has to use the same mule for driver's ed and sex ed!"

10

More Than Meets the Eye

Often mundane-sounding companies are underestimated by Wall Street. The truth is, these operations can be pretty complex, have lots of variables, and produce substantial wealth for investors.

Sanderson Farms

Does a chicken have an immortal soul?

I admit I cringed when one of my students suggested as much to Mike Cockrell, the CFO of Sanderson Farms (SAFM) after our tour of the chicken processor's plant in McComb, Mississippi. (I'm sure that God has a good sense of humor; Mike <u>Cockrell</u> runs the chicken company, Prince <u>Fielder</u> is a major league baseball player...Bernie <u>Madoff</u> "made-off" with all that money!)

It's one of my favorite tours. To start with, the company hatches eggs in giant trays and sends the resulting baby chickens to be raised by farmers in the Mississippi countryside. On their way out the door, the fuzzy baby chicks take a spin on a circular conveyor belt, where they get their vaccinations. It looks like an amusement ride for chickens, like they've gone off to Disney World and a health clinic at the same time. It's easy to fall in love with this first part of the tour, but if you do, you're going to hate the last part.

Weeks later, the grown poultry return in big trucks that back up to the plant. They're commuting, basically. Well, it's kind of a one-way commute. The first room is dark, so as not to alert the chickens to their fate.

About a dozen people in hairnets and shower caps take the chickens and hang them upside down by their feet in stirrups on a conveyor. The conveyor carries the chickens into the plant and drags the chickens' heads across a metal sheet with water running over it. In the next step, they get their throats cut. This is the part of the tale when people say to me "I thought they got away." No, very few get away.

"The chickens seem so calm," one of my students earnestly said to the CFO. "Do you think maybe they find God before they die?" I had just met Mr. Cockrell and was sweating like Britney Spears on Jeopardy!

(I guess in the other 49 states, they would have just slapped him for that. But in Mississippi, folks are just too nice.) "Maybe so," the CFO patiently allowed, "but the other reason might be that the water dunk has an electrical current running through it."

S&P 500 Index vs. Sanderson Farms

Range	12/31/1997	- 06/28/2013	Period	Monthly	No. of Period	186 Month(s)
	Security	Currency	Price Change	Total Return	Difference	Annual Eq
1.	SPX Index	USD	65.52%	121.01%	-680.26%	5.25%
2.	SAFM UW Equity	USD	587.10%	801.26%		15.24%
3.						

1M 3M 6M YTD 1Y 2Y 3Y 5Y 10Y

■ S&P 500 INDEX
☐ SANDERSON FARMS INC

800

600

400

200

0

1998 1999 2000 2001 2002 2003 2004 2005 2006 2007 2008 2009 2010 2011 2012 2013

Total Return

Australia 61 2 9777 8600 Brazil 5511 3048 4500 Europe 44 20 7330 7500 Germany 49 69 9204 1210 Hong Kong 852 2977 6000
Japan 81 3 3201 8900   Singapore 65 6212 1000   U.S. 1 212 318 2000   Copyright 2013 Bloomberg Finance L.P.
SN 774484 EDT GMT-4:00 H433-497-0 22-Jul-2013 18:26:28

Before we got the tour underway, I asked Mike how big the plant was. On my ledger, I have two columns, one for square footage, and one for annual revenue. Mike answered, "Well, this is a big plant, and we kill 1.2 million birds a week at this facility." And I thought, hmmm. I don't have a column for dead birds.

The air is colder in each successive room on the plant tour. That's a good thing, because otherwise some students would get weak in the knees. Everyone is wearing masks and booties, because this plant is pristine.

I've been on a lot of company site visits and I can walk into a building and know what the atmosphere is there. Sometimes you enter the building and quickly sense that everyone hates each other. Or you can walk into a place like Sanderson Farms and realize that they can probably get past rough spots because it's like a family. The company's investor reports always feature employees and their stories, reflecting an important sense of ownership. I'm always taken aback by how long many of these people have worked for Sanderson Farms. Everyone knows each other. Everyone swaps fishing stories. The CFO knows the names of the guys on the line. And when I was there, one of the guys on the line knew him well enough to hear his fish story and then remark, "Mr. Cockrell, I like you, but sometimes you do stretch the truth."

Once I asked Mike how a proposed change in the minimum wage would affect his business. He glanced around at the workers and said, "Do you really think anyone here is working for minimum wage? You can work at McDonald's for minimum wage."

People tell me I'm a nice guy. I really don't have a mean bone in my body. But sometimes I like to assign my prissiest students to this field trip. You know, students who maybe grew up in Manhattan, attended boarding school, and are horrified to discover that their McNuggets don't just magically appear in a cardboard box. This dose of reality is probably good for them, and years later they still talk to me about their site visit. I've actually had students who would not go inside. They were so apprehensive about what they would see inside that they wouldn't get out of the car in the parking lot. I used all my wily ploys and psychiatry skills, and there were some I still couldn't get out of the car!

After the tour, Mike always takes our students across the street to a restaurant called The Dinner Bell, where a featured entree is, of course, chicken. It undoubtedly comes from the plant. The restaurant has a unique set-up, where customers sit around a giant lazy Susan, loaded with platters of delicious Southern comfort food. I always have two equal and opposite reactions to this lazy Susan model. Either every restaurant should be set up like this, or no restaurant should be set up like this.

The stock has been a huge winner and has exceptional management (our students have always been interested in how Mr. Cockrell utilizes both his business and law degrees). Sanderson Farms has done well while other chicken processors have gone out of business. Why? They operate efficiently and have managed to grow without taking on a lot of debt. The management is sharp and they've found a way to keep a family feel, with employees having a sense of ownership, despite the company's growth. They're a long way from the canyons of Wall Street, and in a business that's not considered very sexy. So, they're overlooked and undervalued—just like a lot of other solid regional "stocks under rocks."

People always ask me if I still eat chicken. I do. Sanderson Farms is the cleanest and most efficient operation I have ever seen. And coming from me, the Charles Kurault of plant visitors, that's saying a lot.

Cal-Maine

Cal-Maine Foods (CALM) is in Jackson, Mississippi, which is not exactly a center for publicly traded companies (OK, there are actually three of them). Nevertheless, Cal-Maine is the largest producer and distributor of fresh shell eggs in the United States. If you pick up a carton of eggs at the store and turn it over—keep it closed when you do that—even if it's the store brand, it's probably from Cal-Maine.

S&P 500 Index vs. Cal-Maine

Range 12/31/1997 - 06/28/2013		Period Monthly	No. of Period	186 Month(s)	
Security	Currency	Price Change	Total Return	Difference	Annual Eq
1. SPX Index	USD	65.52%	121.01%	-1762.7%	5.25%
2. CALM UW Equity	USD	1403.35%	1883.68%		21.26%
3.					

Our first report on Cal-Maine listed the company as egg producers. Management later pointed out to us city kids that they were, in fact, egg distributors. "The hens are the actual egg producers!"

When we visited, Fred Adams was the CEO, and Bobby Raines was the CFO. These guys had been running Cal-Maine for decades, and they'd been strategically buying up other egg distributors in the country, to the point where they are now the dominant egg player in the United States.

The office is an older facility that has that 1950s look, it's on Woodrow Wilson Drive in Jackson, and basically it is the complete opposite of what my students at Burkenroad Reports think they are going to experience when they go into finance. They're imagining people working at Google and playing ping-pong and having yoga breaks. This is old school. Nobody is playing ping-pong at the egg factory. But, boy is it profitable!

These tend to be the kinds of places you either work one day and quit, or you are there for 30 years. There is a lot of camaraderie between the management and the line workers.

But following an egg company is a great lesson for students. There's a lot to learn. They realize how seasonal the business is. There are certain baking seasons, such as Thanksgiving, Christmas, and Easter, when egg sales are dramatically higher. Also, demand for eggs, more than for any other product, is constantly at the mercy of medical research. Over the past 20 years, opinion has shifted back and forth, from eggs being bad for you to being good for you.

Now there are free-range eggs, organic eggs, eggs that have less cholesterol, and on and on. Cal-Maine has moved into those areas as well. Specialty eggs are profitable for this company because of its size. To make all of it work on a national level, you need a network of processing plants, because eggs can't be shipped too far.

As a student analyst, you think you have been assigned the world's dullest company, but all of a sudden, you're dealing with the price of corn feed, soy feed, food trends, the surgeon general, labor costs, even Grandma's holiday baking season. They soon begin to think, "I'm creating a forecast here! How many more variables are you going to throw at me?"

So, here's a business that looks simple on the surface, but it's not simple at all. Although it's a well-run, solid business, Cal-Maine has attracted lots of speculators. This isn't a reflection on the company's operation. Instead, Cal-Maine stock has become a vehicle for playing the volatile swings in the prices on corn and soybeans (i.e., chicken feed). Cal-Maine has the most short sellers of any company we follow. These short sellers are betting that Cal-Maine's stock price will fall. The egg business is so closely tied to feed that if the price of feed goes up, it will squeeze the egg company's profit margin. The company won't be able to automatically raise the price of eggs, and in that interim period, profitability can take a tumble.

The size of a company's short position is measured by an esoteric term called "days-to-cover." The calculation takes the number of shares that have been shorted and divides it by the stock's average daily trading volume. As I write this, Cal-Maine has 787,100 shares shorted and an average daily trading volume of 112,000 shares. That gives it a days-to-cover of 5.6 days. That's quite high.

But you can look at this high days-to-cover situation as either bearish OR bullish. It's bearish when you realize that most short selling is done by big, sophisticated players, with a lot of business grads, Bloomberg terminals, you know, armed to the teeth. You think, they're probably right—this is just what they do for a living. Here are smart people, and they're betting against the stock.

It could also be considered a bullish signal because if this stock starts to go up, for whatever reason—declining feed prices, demand, a surgeon general's report—then the people who shorted the sale will get scared, buy their shares back, and send the stock price skyward. This is called a "short squeeze."

You can look at the same data and bet either way, and that's one reason that investing in the stock market is such a great intellectual challenge.

Neither Sanderson Farms nor Cal-Maine is the kind of story that investors salivate over. There's no huge, sexy, game-changing payoff. Instead, these companies offer steady gains that, when compounded, produce very attractive long-term returns. They may not look like home runs, but lots of singles and doubles will add up in the end and make your portfolio a winner.

11

Company Buyouts:
For What it's Worth

If a company keeps posting impressive returns, or its assets are underpriced, eventually even Wall Street will figure it out. This is where buyouts come from.

Here is a list of the 24 Burkenroad companies that have been bought out since we started in 1993:

Year	Company	Buyer	Takeover Premium
1995	Borden Chemical	KKR	+14%
1996	Ambar	Beacon Group	+23%
1997	Melamine Chemicals	Borden Chemicals	+29%
	Ocean Energy*	United Meridian	+8%
1998	Ceanic	Subsea 7	+29%
1999	Avondale Industries	Litton Industries	+27%
	Citation	Kelso	+28%
	Meadowcraft	MWI Acquisition	+88%
2000	Crystal Gas Storage	El Paso	+28%
	KLLM Transport	High Road Acquisition	+15%
2002	ChemFirst	Dupont	+12%
	OSCA	BJ Services	+56%
	JCC Holdings	Harrah's Entertainment	+17%
2003	Ocean Energy	Devon Energy	+3%
	Packaged Ice	Trimaran Partners	+71%
2004	Riviana Foods	Ebro Foods SA	+0%
2006	Sizeler Properties	Revenue Properties	+3%
	Russell Athletic	Berkshire Hathaway	+31%
	Bayou Steel	Black Diamond Capital	+74%
2008	Energy South	Sempra Energy	+33%
2009	NATCO Group	Cameron	+30%
2011	Craftmade Int'l	Litex	+80%
2012	The Shaw Group	CBI	+72%
	McMoRan Exploration	FreeportMcMoRan	+86%

*Merged company kept the Ocean Energy name.

We don't focus on companies we think will be bought out. We focus on strong, well-run companies selling at attractive valuations. These just happen to be the characteristics of companies that attract suitors.

And I'd be remiss if I didn't note that many academic studies show that most mergers don't work out as well as expected. The newlywed companies have to deal with differences in corporate culture, IT systems, leadership, and often increased operating leverage. This is known as "execution risk." Just the name is a bit foreboding!

More Likely to Be Bought Out

When smaller companies get bought out, you are more likely to have a fatter buyout premium. Our companies have been bought out at an average premium of about 35 percent, about in line with the buyout premiums of other small-cap companies (although some of the companies we follow have received buyout premiums that have been much higher). In comparison, takeover premiums on large-cap stocks tend to fall in the 10–20 percent premium range. Investors are always trying to find the next buyout candidate, and you don't have to look very hard to find all the current rumors about who's getting bought out next.

Since the market bottomed out in March 2009, the S&P 500 is up about 150 percent—that's the biggest stock market rally since World War II. Despite that, some stocks still look underpriced, and there are trillions of dollars of cash lying around, earning next to nothing. Some of that cash is destined to be used for acquisitions. One of the easiest ways for a company to grow its earnings is to buy out a competitor, cut out the redundant executive personnel, and benefit from the synergies.

There are a number of reasons that corporate buyouts happen. For example, a buyer might want to expand to an industry where regulation makes it prohibitive or even impossible to start something new.

Or, a company might want to expand its product offerings within its established industry. Another buyer might want to expand its geographical footprint. For these last two scenarios, buyers have to decide if it would be cheaper to start from scratch or to make an acquisition.

As I look at our current crop of stocks, a few companies seem like reasonable buyout candidates. The first might be Cleco Corporation (CNL), a small, well-run utility headquartered in rural central Louisiana, sandwiched between two giant public utilities, Entergy and Southern Co. They have some great coverage areas, strong free cash flow, and are benefiting from very efficient new facilities built over the last decade. It seems as though one of those two big utilities could step up and buy Cleco with the change they find in their respective sofas.

S&P 500 Index vs. Cleco

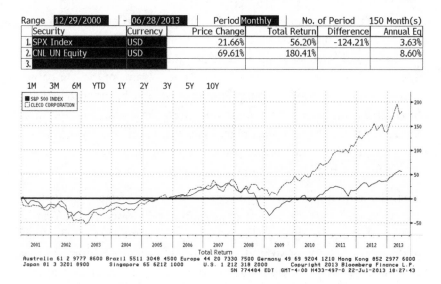

Range 12/29/2000 - 06/28/2013		Period Monthly	No. of Period	150 Month(s)	
Security	Currency	Price Change	Total Return	Difference	Annual Eq
1. SPX Index	USD	21.66%	56.20%	-124.21%	3.63%
2. CNL UN Equity	USD	69.61%	180.41%		8.60%
3.					

Australia 61 2 9777 8600 Brazil 5511 3048 4500 Europe 44 20 7330 7500 Germany 49 69 9204 1210 Hong Kong 852 2977 6000
Japan 81 3 3201 8900   Singapore 65 6212 1000   U.S. 1 212 318 2000   Copyright 2013 Bloomberg Finance L.P.
SN 774484 EDT GMT-4:00 H433-497-0 22-Jul-2013 18:27:43

The company is headquartered in Pineville, Louisiana. Pineville is a little town that is known mainly as the home of the state's mental institution. In the 1940s, Louisiana Governor Earl Long was sent there to "rest and regroup." When he realized he was still the governor, though, he called out the National Guard to free him.

It's still a remote part of the state, and the four-hour trek to Pineville is a real haul for the students in the Burkenroad Reports program.

If Cleco served only rural central Louisiana, it wouldn't be as interesting. But they also provide power to the booming New Orleans bedroom community of St. Tammany Parish. I like to call St. Tammany the fastest-growing parish in the country. Of course, it's a little bit tongue in cheek, since only Louisiana has municipal parishes. But still, it's impressive!

Cleco is a very profitable utility, with an attractive and growing dividend yield. The yield provides investors with a nice return while we wait for a possible buyout to emerge.

Another company that looks like it might be bought out someday is Houston's Powell Industries (POWL). Here's a company that has been around for six decades. They produce equipment and solutions that control and distribute power for such industries as oil and gas, electric utilities, transportation, and water management. Many people would be surprised to know that there are only five analysts that bother to follow the company. They have more than $700 million a year in revenue, and it's exactly the kind of company that would fit neatly into a larger firm serving these industries.

The stock is up about threefold since we first started covering the company in the fall semester 2001.

S&P 500 Index vs. Powell Corp.

Range 12/31/2004 - 06/28/2013	Period Monthly	No. of Period	102 Month(s)			
Security	Currency	Price Change	Total Return	Difference	Annual Eq
1. SPX Index	USD	32.54%	58.98%	-120.36%	5.61%
2. POWL UW Equity	USD	179.34%	179.34%		12.85%
3.					

Total Return
Australia 61 2 9777 8600 Brazil 5511 3048 4500 Europe 44 20 7330 7500 Germany 49 69 9204 1210 Hong Kong 852 2977 6000
Japan 81 3 3201 8900   Singapore 65 6212 1000   U.S. 1 212 318 2000   Copyright 2013 Bloomberg Finance L.P.
                                                          SN 774484 EDT GMT-4:00 H433-497-0 22-Jul-2013 18:28:30

When investors come to our spring conference each year, they're always surprised to find that companies of this caliber seem to be invisible to Wall Street. Stocks like Cleco and Powell may not seem exciting or promise to make an investor very much money over the short term, but if you can buy them and show some patience, they can be quite lucrative. Sometimes it takes a long time for shifts in prices and industry conditions to make the company appealing to a potential buyer.

A lot of times, buyout candidates will be niche players in an industry with much larger competitors. They tend to have good, solid balance sheets—not too much debt that the buyer would have to assume.

Often they represent a piece of the business that is missing from the bigger companies. Take Powell, for example. There are a lot of companies that make electric systems and equipment for big, big projects. And there are many that make equipment for smaller needs. Powell serves the midsize market, and it might be a nice complement to another company.

Another possible buyout candidate is IBERIABANK (IBKC). In 1998, New Orleans-based First National Bank of Commerce (called FNBC by the locals) was bought out by Bank One (this would later be part of JP Morgan Chase). This buyout created big ripples in the region's financial community. Several employees of FNBC's strong money management department left to join Hancock Bank in Gulfport, Mississippi. These are the same folks who launched and manage the Hancock Horizon Burkenroad Small Cap Mutual Fund (HYBUX).

S&P 500 Index vs. IBERIABANK

| Range 12/29/2000 | - 06/28/2013 | Period Monthly | No. of Period | 150 Month(s) |
Security	Currency	Price Change	Total Return	Difference	Annual Eq
1. SPX Index	USD	21.66%	56.20%	-258.67%	3.63%
2. IBKC UW Equity	USD	208.10%	314.87%		12.05%
3.					

Total Return

Australia 61 2 9777 8600 Brazil 5511 3048 4500 Europe 44 20 7330 7500 Germany 49 69 9204 1210 Hong Kong 852 2977 6000
Japan 81 3 3201 8900   Singapore 65 6212 1000   U.S. 1 212 318 2000   Copyright 2013 Bloomberg Finance L.P.
SN 774484 EDT GMT-4:00 H433-497-0 22-Jul-2013 18:29:58

Meanwhile, some of the top executives of FNBC went over to run tiny Lafayette, Louisiana-based IBERIABANK. To say that this was a couple of small buildings and a ticker symbol would not be a real stretch. This new management has turned IBERIABANK into a banking power-house running from Texas to Florida. While most banks raced to open branches and make loans in Florida in the mid-2000's, IBERIABANK got its toehold in the state *after* the real estate bust and purchased many of its Florida operations from the FDIC at bargain prices. It operates in one of the fastest-growing parts of the country and looks like an attractive target for a bigger national bank.

Being a Public Company: Good? Bad? or Ugly?

Years ago, most entrepreneurs hoped to eventually bring their companies public. It was the "Holy Grail." The IPO would make you a very wealthy person, and running a public company was the ultimate status symbol.

That is just not the case anymore. Since the Enron debacle, two things have happened that make taking a company public much less attractive. One is the Sarbanes-Oxley Act, which tightened oversight over public companies and made top management accountable for the accuracy of financial information. There is just so much more scrutiny now, and so much more paperwork. It has been helpful in restoring investor confidence, but it's been particularly hard (and expensive) for smaller companies. Sarbanes-Oxley has put people who run these companies on the hook. The CFO and CEO sign off on the financials, and if something is not right, they could do time in the Big House. Board members too are on the hook if anything untoward is going on, financially or legally.

There are some real drawbacks to being a public company. Managers have to run their businesses on a three-month timeline. If you beat the estimates all the time, analysts say you were lowballing them. If you don't make the estimates, God help you, they will fry you and leave you. And that's what happened to many companies.

And public companies have to disclose ANY significant news. I'll always remember visiting with the CFO of a newly public oil company in Louisiana. He told us about the company having drilled a particularly expensive and soul-deflating dry hole and how the firm's legal department demanded that they issue a press release on it (he would have preferred to just skulk away and move on to the next project). On the flip side, the company had also made a significant discovery and would have liked to buy up the surrounding properties before word got out (no chance!).

It used to be that once executives reached a certain age, their retirement plan was to do some fishing, play a bit of golf, and get a friend to put them on the board of a publicly traded company. But now boards strive to have truly "independent" directors, and sitting on a public board is such an obligation and can be such a liability, that good directors are hard to find.

So, the company that once might have viewed going public as the next logical step doesn't see it that way anymore. Those companies that are already publicly traded mumble about just going private. As a result, small and microcap companies are getting bought out, and fewer new companies are coming up to replace them.

After one of our Burkenroad Reports investment conferences, a guy came up to talk to me. He was an executive of one of the biggest companies in Louisiana. He said, "Half of these companies shouldn't be public. They are too small; they get all the negatives of being public, like costs and liability, and they're not getting any of the positives." Publicly traded companies have shareholders and analysts who are constantly bugging them about quarterly results and forcing them into a short-term mindset, which is not good for running a business.

Furthermore, the reason you went public in the first place was that you wanted great access to capital. You wanted your shares to be that currency to buy other companies with. But many executives feel that their shares are being undervalued in the market and don't want to give them up at these levels!

The Urge to Merge

When I look at the stock market these days, I can't help but think about a funny old routine by Father Guido Sarducci: the Five Minute University. The concept was that in five minutes—and for $20—he could teach you what the average college graduate remembers five years after graduating from college. When he gets to economics, he looks out at the audience with a knowing smile.

"Supply and demand," he says, nodding his head. "That's it."

Father Sarducci was really onto something. When it comes to the stock market, it really is all about supply and demand, and while most investors tend to think there's an unlimited supply of stocks, that's not really the case. The reality is the supply of shares available for purchase by investors has been steadily declining over the past several years.

Undervalued stock prices, low interest rates, and easy access to capital have fed a truly amazing buyout binge. It's hard to believe, but there are now 45 percent fewer public companies trading in the Wilshire 5000 than there were 12 years ago. (About 3,000 stocks (net) have disappeared since the year 2000.)

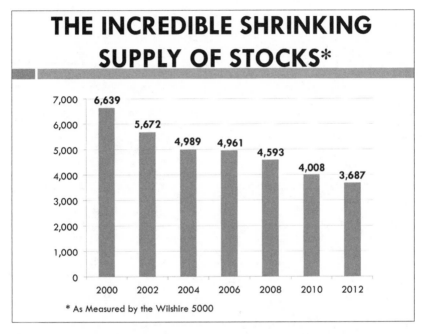

THE INCREDIBLE SHRINKING SUPPLY OF STOCKS*

* As Measured by the Wilshire 5000

Add this to the surge in share buybacks discussed earlier, and it's certainly a bullish factor for the share prices of the remaining publicly traded companies! What does this all mean for investors? As any student of economics can tell you, a smaller pool of shares available for purchase by individual and institutional investors should lead to higher prices. Companies will continue to buy back their own shares until they feel that those shares are fully valued by the marketplace.

It's more dollars chasing fewer shares. Supply and demand. That's something that even a graduate of the Five Minute University can understand. Ciao!

12

Market Mythbusters

Unlike the television show "Mythbusters" (one of my favorites), I'm sorry to say that we won't be blowing things up in this chapter. Darn budget constraints! But I would like to explode some of the major myths that keep people out of the stock market at exactly the wrong time.

MYTHBUSTER THOUGHT NO. 1: The four most dangerous words in finance are "this time it's different!"

It's never different. It's just capitalism, and it's a naturally cyclical economic system. (Now, the seven most dangerous words are probably "Hey, we're getting the band back together!")

You tend to hear these proclamations when stocks are selling at either insanely bullish or insanely bearish valuations. In the financial meltdown of 2008–2009, fear levels were so high that you simply couldn't reason with investors. The severe decline in stock prices allowed investors to purchase shares at the lowest valuations in a generation. On the flip side, in 1999–2000, the valuations on the market (particularly tech stocks) beggared belief. Investors clamored for ownership in Silicon Valley companies that had no earnings, no assets, and no cash flow. Who knew?

In the summer of 1999, I was giving a talk to 400 money managers at Hilton Head, South Carolina. Speakers before me had preached that the traditional stock valuation metrics were no longer useful and that it was "a new paradigm" (another way of saying "This time it's different."). Just before I went on the stage, the conference sponsor pulled me aside and said, "I know how you feel about the current market, but could you just go out there and say something positive?" I asked if he would accept two negatives. The tech-heavy NASDAQ has never fully recovered from the dot-com bust that soon followed.

I teach the old-fashioned Ben Graham/Warren Buffett kind of fundamental analysis, based on earnings and balance sheets, and in the 1999–2000 period, I looked like some kind of dinosaur in the classroom. I remember when an undergraduate approached me after class and said, "I'm looking at this stock my friend Josh told me about, and I'm checking out what we covered in class, and I noticed it doesn't have a PE"—or Price to Earnings ratio. Exasperated by the current market's disconnect with traditional valuation metrics, I uttered, "There's a reason for that Jimmy.... It has no E"! Oh, those were rough times to be teaching about value investing. I was an angry old Italian guy walking around campus. ("Hey, say something in Italian." "Sure! The body's in the trunk!" Oh boy, my Dad wouldn't have wanted me telling that joke.)

(Question: "Why don't Italians like the Jehovah's Witnesses?" Answer: "We don't like any witnesses!" OK, I'll stop.)

The truth is, the stock market (as measured by the Standard and Poors 500 index) rises in price on about 75 percent of the days that it is open. Since 1926, the stock market has provided an annual total return of just about 10 percent. Over long periods of time (I know, Keynes said that in the long run, we're all dead), stocks have outperformed just about every other asset class, including real estate and bonds.

And here's a little "inside baseball" on money management. Money managers don't usually get fired by clients for being fully invested in stocks during a declining market. These investors made an asset allocation and gave that money to the manager to gain exposure to that particular area. However, managers do get fired by clients for having too much in cash (and out of the stock market) during a rising market. This creates another upward bias to stock prices and verifies the mantra that it's safer to be in the market than out.

Back up and look at this long-term stock performance chart from across the room. (This gets harder as you get older.)

S&P 500 Index (1927–2013)

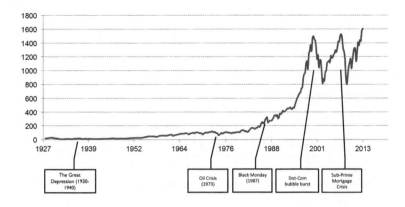

The downturns and disasters of the past just don't seem so catastrophic when you look at the long run. Close up, while you're in the middle of them, they look like the end of the world. If you back up, you can see that these "corrections" weren't really much of anything.

MYTHBUSTER THOUGHT NO. 2: If the majority of people were right, the majority of people would be rich. There's an old line from Wall Street—"You pay a high price for a cheery consensus." In other words, by the time all of your fellow investors are in agreement that stocks are a great investment, the stocks are probably no longer a bargain. It's better to be bullish when the street is still full of bears.

For example, in the 1990s, two thirds of Americans felt that the country was on the wrong track. It turns out that the 1990s was a great time to be invested in the stock market.

Then in 2000, 80 percent of Americans felt the country was on the right track, and yet we fell into the lost decade, in terms of the stock market.

In 2010, nearly everyone felt the country was "on the wrong track." Yet since 2010, the market has gone practically straight up. It is uncanny how you have to swim against the tide to make money in the stock market.

Swim upstream. Be the salmon!

MYTHBUSTER THOUGHT NO. 3: Donkey pride.

The myth here is that you shouldn't be in the stock market when Democrats are in the White House. Republicans are viewed as pro-business, and therefore, investors reason, the market should do better when there is a Republican president.

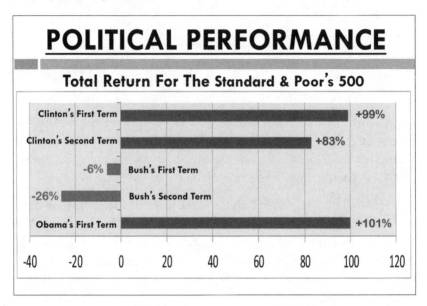

POLITICAL PERFORMANCE

Total Return For The Standard & Poor's 500

Clinton's First Term	+99%
Clinton's Second Term	+83%
-6%	Bush's First Term
-26%	Bush's Second Term
Obama's First Term	+101%

-40   -20   0   20   40   60   80   100   120

Well, I was born at night...but not last night!

The fact is that historically, stocks have done better when a Democrat was in the White House. In the past 20 years, this trend has been amplified to insane levels.

MYTHBUSTER THOUGHT NO. 4: Stay out of the stock market when unemployment is high.

Now, this makes sense...UNLESS YOU THINK ABOUT IT! It's actually just the opposite. Since 1948, stock returns are more than three times higher when unemployment rates have been ABOVE 6.6 percent.

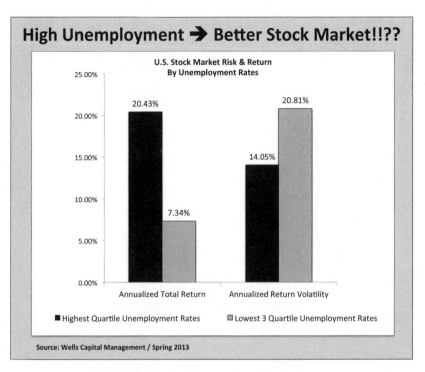

High Unemployment → Better Stock Market!!??

U.S. Stock Market Risk & Return
By Unemployment Rates

- Highest Quartile Unemployment Rates
- Lowest 3 Quartile Unemployment Rates

Source: Wells Capital Management / Spring 2013

Why? Sure it sounds a bit counterintuitive, but when unemployment is high, the government is under pressure to get people back to work. The Federal Reserve will lower interest rates and hold them down, and the government will start spending money on big projects to stimulate the economy. That's exactly what the stock market and corporate America want.

These points go a long way in explaining why the "average investor" earns returns that are, well, far "below average." Add this to the fact that most investors:

- Aren't diversified.

- Don't have a financial game plan and tend to buy rumors or hot stocks they hear about from "friends" or through the financial media.

- Are speculators, not investors, and lack patience.

Take all this into account, and it's not hard to see why most people have an uninspiring (or worse) experience investing in stocks.

13

Celebrities and Prognosticators

Great Experiences

Burkenroad Reports has been very fortunate to have received wonderful coverage in the national media over the past 20 years. This has given me some terrific opportunities, like my two appearances in *The Wall Street Journal's* "Dartboard Stock Picking Contest." Here, four money managers are asked to pick one stock they think will do well over the next six months. Not only are you competing against your fellow stock experts, but you also need to beat the four darts that have been winged against a dartboard covered with the stock pages.

This, of course, goes against everything I teach in class, as six months isn't a long-term investment and one stock doesn't make a diversified portfolio. And it also shows that following recommendations in the financial media doesn't necessarily lead to the Promised Land. In each contest, I have finished fourth out of four money managers and have lost to the darts! However, after the games were over, both of my stocks were bought out and their prices rose substantially.

I've also been a guest several times on the national PBS program the Nightly Business Report. Out of Miami, this is the granddaddy of financial programs. Anchor Tom Hudson was talking to me about the results of the Burkenroad Fund and caught me a bit off guard when he stated, "I think your students are smart—but you're also fishing in the right pond." I had to admit that small, under-followed, profitable companies...yeah, that's the best place to bait your hook.

Jim Cramer

In the fall semester of 2010, famed CNBC "Mad Money" host Jim Cramer came to do his show on campus. Cramer is a folk hero among the nation's business school students and the school was abuzz! His high-energy show has done so much to increase interest in the markets and stock selection.

A lot of planning goes into that show, and a couple of weeks before the taping CNBC sent a big, furry, red bull mascot to my classroom. (I assume there was a human being in there.) The bull squeezed into a desk in my Burkenroad Reports class to tape a promotional piece they were doing for the show. The next week, Cramer and his crew came to campus. He turned out to be a very kind, soft-spoken man—contrary to his TV persona—who was very appreciative of the Tulane sweatshirts we gave him (it must have worked; his daughter is now a Tulane student). But once the camera's red light went on, it was "BOO-YAH BABY!" The whole thing was very cool.

Liam Kelly, a student in the Burkenroad program, takes on "Mad Money" host Jim Cramer on the stock of McMoRan Exploration, an oil and gas exploration company with big potential in the shallow waters of coastal Louisiana. We called this stock idea "Finding Alpha in the Delta."

Three of my Burkenroad students pitched their stock ideas to him on the show. He was tough but fair as he and the students went toe-to-toe on TV. It was the opportunity of a lifetime for these students, and I'm pleased to say that they are all working in the investment business today. The students from this program graduate with exceptional real-world skills, and Burkenroad Reports has been a wonderful career springboard (say what you will about working in finance, but there's no heavy lifting, and most of the work is indoors!).

Warren Buffett

Just a few days after the closing of Lehman Brothers (a.k.a, "The End of the World") in October 2008, I brought 27 of my students to Omaha, Nebraska, to spend the day with investing legend Warren Buffett. The trip had been planned for months. I always felt that Buffett liked what we were doing with small, overlooked stocks, as that is how he started in the investment field. He now manages so much money that he needs to focus on big name, large cap stocks.

I do a lot of public speaking and meet a lot of famous people, and sometimes when I get to know them, I'm kind of non-plussed. But Warren Buffett blew me away. He was wise, funny, and very generous with his time.

After visiting his Nebraska Furniture Mart store and his Borsheims Jewelry store, we went to his (nice but humbly appointed) office for a couple of hours of Q&A. Then it was off to lunch with the man himself. While the rest of my students headed to the waiting bus, Stephen Frapart, the student who secured both the Jim Cramer and Warren Buffett visits, yelled "shotgun" and got to ride alongside Mr. Buffett to nearby Piccolo's restaurant (I thought to myself, that kid's going places!).

After lunch, we presented Buffett with a customized baseball bat to commemorate our visit. He had the patience of Job as we all lined up for photos with him. At one point, he handed me back the bat and suggested that I just put it in his car. As a few of my students and I walked down the street to his car, we began to think, "His car is open? The wealthiest man on the planet doesn't lock his car?"

The author and Warren Buffett (he's on the right; OK, you knew that).

Yup, I opened the back door and put the baseball bat alongside his umbrella on the back seat of his Lincoln Town Car. I had to open the car door, as my students thought that it must be booby-trapped.

At a time when everyone else on Wall Street was in a panic, Warren Buffett was calm and insightful.

He noted that as corporations and individuals were de-leveraging, the government would have no choice other than to up their leverage.

It was the midst of the housing market collapse. Buffett said the big problem was that there were just too many homes out there. The glut would have to work its way through the economic system and be absorbed over time. Buffett joked that we could solve the situation a lot more quickly by just "blowing up" 1.5 million homes. But, which homes would get the TNT treatment? These issues would stir some debate!

That very same day, his now famous editorial appeared in *The New York Times*. He urged calm and said that stocks were being offered today at very attractive prices for the long-term investor. He was skillfully fighting off the mantra of those days: "This time it's different! It's time to panic!"

In retrospect, he was spot on.

I liked his approach. Generally, I am more predisposed to listen to long-term ideas, because I think short-term movements in stocks are random, while long-term investment themes are more predictable (and profitable).

The final question came from a student who asked, "How bad is it on Wall Street these days?" Mr. Buffett paused, and then told this story:

> "I heard that when the stock market crashed last Friday, an investment banker left his office, went home to his big house on Long Island, met his wife at the door, and told her, 'Honey, we've got to talk.'
>
> "'It looks like I'm not going to get a bonus this year, and honey, I may not get a bonus next year. So darling, I hate to even bring this up, but you're going to have to learn to cook, because we're going to have to fire the chef.'
>
> "She looked him in the eye and replied, 'Darling, then you'll have to learn to make love, because we're going to have to get rid of the gardener.'"

I love that guy.

Stock-Picking: A Lost Art

Nowadays, stock ideas don't even come up in conversation much. Most people know what I do, but rarely am I approached for my opinion anymore at cocktail parties, barbecues, or crawfish boils (those social gatherings in South Louisiana where locals line up over newspaper-covered tables and tear apart small crustaceans for the spicy morsels within).

On my weekly radio show, I ask each guest for a stock pick. Getting an answer can be like pulling teeth. Many guests (and they're all business people) tell me they don't follow stocks, and the ones that do offer me the same few each week (i.e., Apple, Amazon, Google...). I also get the fringe investment ideas such as Iraqi dinars, viatical settlements, and antique gold coins. Gold is advertised on late-night TV and, well, historically the things I have bought on late-night TV have usually not worked out!

I think that the dot.com bust of 1999–2000 and the financial meltdown of 2008–2009 may have ruined an entire generation of investors. In fact, the financial network CNBC is currently experiencing its lowest ratings in 20 years. Even my students seem a bit gun shy these days. Skepticism is a good quality in an analyst or investor, but many students seem to systematically underestimate the financial performance and stock appreciation potential of the companies we follow. Even after meeting with an exciting, well-positioned company, some students remain unimpressed.

As a contrarian investor, I take today's lack of interest in the markets as a signal that there are still opportunities out there.

14

Crunching Numbers

Let's face it, most of us learned math from a vampire made of felt on "Sesame Street" (you remember "The Count!"). Here's where some basic stock market math comes in, and I'm going to stick with a bikini format—covering the essential parts with a minimum of material.

Heck, we're the country that invented math anxiety. (They say most of us are using only 20 percent of our brain. Sometimes it makes me wonder what I am doing with the other 70 percent.) There are some numbers and calculations that are very helpful to the investor. The math isn't complex, and most of the figures are readily available on the Internet on sites such as Yahoo! Finance.

There are several ways to value a stock, and I think that the best way to show these calculations is to apply them to an actual company.

P/E Ratio

I've chosen to look at P/E through AFC Enterprises (AFCE). You probably don't know them by this name. Its stores are called Popeyes Chicken & Biscuits. The company was founded by flamboyant New Orleans entrepreneur Al Copeland. Kentucky Fried Chicken is bigger but is a part of gigantic YUM! Brands, which includes other food operators such as Taco Bell and Pizza Hut and has 24 analysts following their stock. AFCE is covered by just five analysts. And this is very subjective, of course, but nobody in New Orleans would be caught with a box of anything but Popeyes fried chicken while watching a Mardi Gras parade!

They operate more than 2,000 restaurants in 28 countries, and the chain has undergone quite a revival since Cheryl Bachelder stepped in as the company's CEO in 2007.

When you look at a company's financials, you almost always see them on a per-share basis. That makes it easy to compare the performance of companies that are very different. This is the basis of an important figure called the Price/Earnings ratio, or P/E for short. (If you still think P/E is gym class, go to jail, do not pass go, and do not collect $200!)

The P/E is a simple calculation. Divide the stock price by the earnings per share. The result is sometimes called "the multiple." The higher the P/E, the more enthusiastic investors are about the fortunes of the company. If you had a stock that sold at $20 a share, and the earnings per share is $2, the P/E is 10. If the earnings per share on the same stock is $1, the P/E is 20! (Or put another way, the stock sells at a price 20 times its earnings per share.)

Price Per Share

—————————— = Price/Earnings Ratio*

Earnings Per Share*

> * When we use the most recent four quarters (trailing earnings), we call that a "trailing P/E." When we use the forecast earnings for the next 12 months, that is referred to as a "forward P/E."

As an investor, you must keep your eye on earnings. It's usually the single most important variable.

S&P 500 Index vs. AFC Enterprises

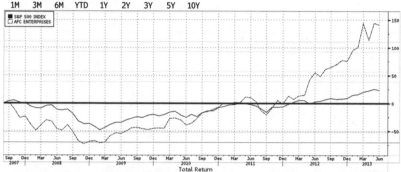

Range	08/31/2007	-	06/28/2013	Period	Monthly	No. of Period	70 Month(s)
	Security		Currency	Price Change		Total Return	Difference	Annual Eq
1.	SPX Index		USD	8.98%		23.99%	-117.06%	3.76%
2.	AFCE UW Equity		USD	141.05%		141.05%		16.29%
3.								

1M   3M   6M   YTD   1Y   2Y   3Y   5Y   10Y

■ S&P 500 INDEX
□ AFC ENTERPRISES

Total Return

Australia 61 2 9777 8600 Brazil 5511 3048 4500 Europe 44 20 7330 7500 Germany 49 69 9204 1210 Hong Kong 852 2977 6000
Japan 81 3 3201 8900   Singapore 65 6212 1000   U.S. 1 212 318 2000   Copyright 2013 Bloomberg Finance L.P.
SN 774484 EDT GMT-4:00 G457-2908-1 07-Aug-2013 17:34:06

AFC Enterprises (7/5/2013)

- EPS last 12 months: $1.29

- EPS projected for the next 12 months: $1.49

- Trailing: 29.0x

- Forward: 25.6x

As I write this, the stock market (as measured by the S&P 500) is selling at 15.5 times next year's expected earnings. The forward P/E for AFC Enterprises, 25.6, is about 70 percent higher than that of today's overall market, and this would indicate that investors have already "priced in" some pretty exciting growth prospects from the company.

Since 1990, the market has sold at an average P/E of about 16.5 times forward earnings.

IS THIS MARKET CHEAP?

S&P 500 Forward P/E

Median = 16.5x

Source: FactSet, Standard & Poor's, as of June 28, 2013

Historic P/E of the market.

People say a stock goes up when there are more buyers than sellers. A better answer may be that a stock goes up when the company exceeds expectations. It goes down when its results disappoint investors.

I've heard people suggest buying stock in retailers in November because Christmas is their busiest time of year. Well, this is true. (The day after Thanksgiving is termed "Black Friday" because that's the day most retailers finally begin operating in the black.) But everyone knows this, and in order for these stocks to rise, the stores need to be more than busy. They need to earn more money than Wall Street was expecting.

If you look at it that way, you want to find a company with very low expectations. We like to find companies where if people just show up for work, they beat expectations. A high P/E means that there's already a lot expected of a company.

Thoughts on P/E

- The higher the expected growth rate of the company's earnings, the higher the P/E ratio is.

- Another factor is the balance sheet. Generally, investors will pay a higher multiple for a company that is in good financial shape.

- Similar stocks tend to sell at roughly the same P/E ratio. Chevron and Exxon, for example, are going to sell at about the same P/E ratio. A high-tech company might sell at a P/E of 50 because the growth potential is so high, relative to what they are doing now. On the other hand, an old-line food stock might sell at a P/E of just 10, because its earnings can't grow very fast.

Finding the Catalyst

In class, when students pitch me a stock idea, the first question I ask them is, "What is going to make the stock price go higher?" In other words, what is the catalyst here? The students do a great job digging up information, but unless that data translates into higher earnings per share or a higher P/E multiple, it's hard to argue for making an investment.

There are only three possible answers. Here are the scenarios to get a rise in the stock price:

A. Earnings can show steady growth, because the management is strong and there's a real need for the product.

B. It's not loved (or even known very well) on the street. If the stock catches the eyes of additional analysts and investors, it could give a boost to its P/E ratio. What we often find is that there are many stocks that sell at low valuations but simply don't have the catalyst needed to bring up share prices. We jokingly refer to these stocks as "perma-cheaps."

C. Some combination of A & B. Here you could have a situation where the earnings and the P/E could go up, and that could give the stock a real lift.

PEG Ratio

Here we'll take a look at Houston Wire & Cable (HWCC). This well-run company serves as the middleman for specialty electrical wire and cable between electrical distributors and cable manufacturers. Despite

the Lone Star moniker, it operates nationwide, has a solid 35-year rep-
utation in the business, and is known for its broad and deep region-
ally profiled inventory. I consider the stock a barometer of the nation's
overall economic health. (Oh, and if you're ever looking for those cool
wooden spools to use as a coffee table in a dorm, well, that's what the
wire comes on, and they've got plenty of them.) We have been writing
about Houston Wire & Cable since 2010, and still only four analysts are
following the stock.

S&P 500 Index vs. Houston Wire & Cable

Range	12/31/2009	- 06/28/2013		Period Monthly	No. of Period	42 Month(s)
	Security	Currency	Price Change	Total Return	Difference	Annual Eq
1.	SPX Index	USD	44.05%	55.07%	26.09%	13.38%
2.	HWCC UW Equity	USD	16.30%	28.98%		7.56%
3.						

1M 3M 6M YTD 1Y 2Y 3Y 5Y 10Y

S&P 500 INDEX
HOUSTON WIRE & CABLE CO

Total Return

Australia 61 2 9777 8600 Brazil 5511 3048 4500 Europe 44 20 7330 7500 Germany 49 69 9204 1210 Hong Kong 852 2977 6000
Japan 81 3 3201 8900   Singapore 65 6212 1000   U.S. 1 212 318 2000   Copyright 2013 Bloomberg Finance L.P.
                                                SN 774484 EDT GMT-4:00 G457-2908-1 07-Aug-2013 17:33:15

The basic premise of the PEG ratio is to find companies with projected
growth rates that are high relative to their P/E valuation. We divide the
P/E ratio by the projected growth rate, and we are ideally trying to find
stocks with PEGs of 1.00 or below. That means we're not overpaying
for the company's growth potential. It's pretty easy to find a stock with
a low P/E, but the PEG ratio offers a bit more insight. Maybe the stock
has a very low P/E, but maybe there's a good reason for that. The PEG
ratio will tell you.

Houston Wire & Cable (7/3/2013)

Trailing P/E Ratio: 15.0x

Projected Growth Rate: 16.0x

PEG Ratio: 0.97x

The growth rate is a prediction made by analysts who gather as much information as they can about the stock and all the factors affecting it. Analysts are getting paid to forecast the future, and you can find their estimates on several investment websites.

The PEG for Houston Wire & Cable came in at 0.97x. That's below 1.00, and this piques our interest. One popular style of investing is called GARP. The GARP investor is willing to pay up for "growth at a reasonable price," and the PEG ratio is a good valuation tool for these folks.

Enterprise Value/EBITDA

Enterprise Value divided by EBITDA is an important measure of a stock's valuation.

I've chosen to look at Enterprise Value/EBITDA through a company called RPC, Inc. (RES). RPC is a longtime Burkenroad company that serves the oilfield with a variety of services and had seen several big swings in its share price since we began following it in 2001. The company has grown a lot over the years, and would now actually be considered a mid cap stock. One of the services that RPC is known for is the handling of oil well fires and blow-outs. Think John Wayne in "Hellfighters"!

Here's how Enterprise Value/EBITDA works. The numerator, Enterprise Value, is what it would cost you to actually buy a company. It's the market capitalization plus all the debt the company owes, minus its cash and marketable securities.

Here's how you calculate Enterprise Value:

(Share Price x Number of Shares Outstanding) + (Total Debt - Cash and Marketable Securities)

For RPC, Inc. (7/5/2013)

Share Price:	$14.06
Shares Outstanding:	220,560,000
Total Debt:	$87,600,000
Cash & Marketable Securities:	$10,280,000
Enterprise Value:	$3,178,400,000

Now let's take a look at the denominator, EBITDA.

EBITDA basically measures the cash flow or, to be precise and to explain the initials, the "earnings before interest, taxes, depreciation, and amortization." Put another way, EBITDA measures the company's operating cash flow and is a good method by which to compare companies.

Most analysts feel more comfortable using EBITDA (or cash flow) than Earnings Per Share (EPS) because earnings per share can be easily manipulated. Depreciation, the sale of assets, and other financial maneuvers can alter EPS and mask how well the company is actually doing. RPC's most recent EBITDA comes to $592,240,000.

This gives the stock an EV/EBITDA of 5.3x. An attractive EV/EBITDA can differ from industry to industry, but this looks to be very reasonable. We like to see stocks where the number is below 8.

S&P 500 Index vs. RPC Inc.

Range 12/29/2000	- 06/28/2013	Period Monthly	No. of Period	150 Month(s)	
Security	Currency	Price Change	Total Return	Difference	Annual Eq
1. SPX Index	USD	21.66%	55.10%	-959.24%	3.57%
2. RES UN Equity	USD	814.91%	1014.34%		21.26%
3.					

1M   3M   6M   YTD   1Y   2Y   3Y   5Y   10Y

■ S&P 500 INDEX
☐ RPC INC

Total Return

Australia 61 2 9777 8600 Brazil 5511 3048 4500 Europe 44 20 7330 7500 Germany 49 69 9204 1210 Hong Kong 852 2977 6000
Japan 81 3 3201 8900   Singapore 65 6212 1000   U.S. 1 212 318 2000   Copyright 2013 Bloomberg Finance L.P.
SN 774484 EDT GMT-4:00 G457-2908-1 07-Aug-2013 17:25:30

A Little Story About Enterprise Value

Enterprise Value (EV) is a metric you can find on the Internet. It's also something we started including in each Burkenroad Report, and here's the story behind that decision.

There's a global network of young business leaders that is open to people who are both presidents of significant companies and under 50 years of age. It is a big "movers and shakers" kind of thing, but for younger movers and shakers. They have meetings where they educate, share ideas, and so on.

Some members of the Louisiana chapter were somewhat surprised that when they turned 50, they were "disinvited" from the group. So, they decided to keep getting together, even if they were really just getting together for drinks and fellowship, but for the sake of appearances at least they planned an educational component, and one year that was me.

I got an invitation saying they were going to have a meeting, and could I come talk about Burkenroad Reports. They met in the coolest place: a beautiful house on the batture, which is the strip of land tucked away on the Mississippi River side of the levee. I hoisted my canvas bag full of Burkenroad compendiums, climbed the green, grassy levee, and walked up a rickety gangplank. I opened the door, and there were all these multi-millionaires in the room.

It was a beautiful house, in a guy's kind of way, like the best clubhouse ever. The porch was right on the river, and there was a rubber alligator made out of tire tread on the kitchen counter—this house was what a guy would buy if he had some money in his pocket and his wife didn't have any say.

The ships turn on the river there, about 200 feet from the porch. I was watching the huge ocean-going ships come straight toward me before they turned, and inside I was thinking, hmm, we are all going to die here! (Of course, these big tankers are expertly steered and pivot harmlessly upriver every time.)

There was a nice lunch, and then it was time to speak. I handed out a book of one-page reports on all the companies we followed. I launched into my spiel about a company that owns four shipyards in Louisiana and Texas, where they build and repair ships, barges, and even passenger ferries. That was Conrad Industries out of Morgan City (CNRD), and the stock was doing well, as I told my listeners.

One of the guys, looking over the report, reached for his drink and asked me, "How much does it cost?" I said $6 a share. He said, "Naw, son. The whole thang." Boys and girls, in his self-made-millionaire way, he was asking about the company's "enterprise value."

The Lower, the Better

Low P/E ratios, low PEGs, and low EV/EBITDA ratios are what true value investors want to see. These metrics are especially helpful when comparing stocks for their relative attractiveness. Value investing often takes a lot of patience. It may take other investors a long while to recognize what you have discovered.

15

Kicking Tires

I love finding and researching public companies. There are many attributes that are helpful here, but none as much as curiosity. I was always curious. I was that kid in Sunday School likely to ask, "But Father, if Jesus really were a Jew, why the Spanish name?" Curiosity is a good trait, but, oooh, the rulers hurt!

Each spring, we host the Burkenroad Reports Investment Conference. Executives from most of the companies we follow make presentations about the outlook for their companies and industries. It's free and open to the public and attracts about 700 investors each year. OK, it's always on the first Friday of the Jazz & Heritage Festival (www.jazzfest.com) and that helps bring in people too! The conference also serves as a showcase for the research reports published by our students (the reports and student produced videos are also available free of charge on our website at www.burkenroad.org).

Whether you meet them during a breakout session at a conference like our Burkenroad Reports or contact them on your own, the smart small investor will find it useful to talk to managers at the companies where you're thinking about buying stock.

At smaller companies, you might get a chance to talk to the CEO, but probably the person you are looking for is the chief financial officer. Usually, the chief financial officer is a CPA, and most of them have previously worked at one of the Big Four accounting firms. A lot of times, they were auditing that company and someone in management said,

"How would you like to stop living in motels, settle down, and have a family? Come work for us."

When meeting with large-cap companies, you tend to meet an investor relations person with a $1,500 suit and a PowerPoint presentation deck. But with smaller companies, we're more likely to sit down with management and the people who built the company. Here you get some pretty shoot-from-the-hip answers. I had one student ask an oil company's founder (he was in his late 70s), "How will you be doing next year if oil prices stay above $90 a barrel?" and the founder replied, "Above $90 a barrel, and I'll be farting through silk." Not a quote you would find in a press release, but definitely insightful, and memorable.

The CFO should be an accountant, but that same person also needs to be creative and a problem solver. A CFO at a public company wears many hats, including speaking to shareholders, portfolio managers, and analysts, as well as designing PowerPoint presentations and annual reports. That person, at a small public company, is always a bit overworked. His or her role is a left brain/right brain kind of combination. They may be more receptive to calls than you would think. They probably have a great story to tell about the company if they could just get someone to listen.

In 2000, Congress passed Regulation Fair Disclosure (more commonly known as Reg FD). It basically says that companies can't share any meaningful information with one person that has not been offered to everyone. This sometimes makes my students a bit nervous about speaking to management. I still laugh thinking about a visit we had with a billboard company in the 1990s. The company had grown through a series of buyouts, and one of my undergraduate students asked the executive how much they were targeting for acquisitions next year. After he told her, she followed up with "Can you tell me the companies you plan to buy?" He responded, "I would, but then I'd have to kill you!"

Don't worry. Nobody goes to prison for asking questions. It's answering questions that can be the problem. There are real consequences here, and management is on their toes.

The students prepare very good questions, and I also bring a list of inquiries. Don't start your questions with a verbose preamble just to make yourself look smart. Also, don't waste their valuable time by asking questions that could be answered by looking at the company website.

Instead, look for hidden factors. For example, I once brought my students to visit the executives at Crown Crafts (CRWS), which is the world's largest player in what they call the "juvenile industry"—baby supplies such as bibs and crib bedding. In trying to develop a forecast of future sales, my students were relying on predictions of the U.S. birthrate. However, the CEO pointed out that it's a little narrower than that. The real driver, he said, is the rate of FIRST births. When families have a second or third kid, they use the same bibs they bought for the firstborn. That's insight you can use.

Start with open-ended questions that get a conversation started. I usually start by asking "What keeps you up at night?" After a giggle and some reference to their lifestyle, management will open up about the issues and challenges facing the company.

Another good open-ended question for us is, "We plan to speak with your competitors. What will they say about you?" They might start with "Uh, that we're bastards!" and then go on to explain how the industry works, where they fit in, and what niche markets they compete in.

Other good questions include the following:[*]

- Where are you looking for potential new growth? What will this company look like five years from now?

- Are management compensation programs aligned with shareholders' interests? Are they tied to performance, and is there some "glue in the seat"? (I love this expression. It refers to delayed vesting incentives to keep key personnel at the company.)

- What should we monitor in order to track the progress of your objectives?

[*] *Tom Putnam (Tulane MBA-1968) and CEO of Fenimore Asset Management, supplied us with these insightful questions more than a decade ago. Thanks, Tom.*

If you go to a company's website, you can see their next scheduled conference call. You can call in, listen, and even ask questions. What you are going to find is that many of the questions you have will be voiced by other investors and analysts. Another good source is the archived conference calls stored on the company's website. I like to go back and listen to the last two or three calls and see if what management predicted and promised has come to fruition. If management are without a strategy and timeline and are always just "putting out fires," that's a bad sign.

I also hope to find this continuity when I read the company's last few annual reports. The president's letter is usually valuable reading. The first half of the letter is a look back at the trials and tribulations of the past year. The second half should lay out their strategies and goals for the following 12 months.

There's one source of information you should probably steer clear of, and that's online message boards. There's at least one for nearly every public company. It always seems to me that the comments come from bitter ex-employees of the company or people with little insight and lots of time on their hands (probably living in their parents' basements). They talk a big game but probably aren't substantial investors and don't have any real insight—or, as they like to say in Texas, "all hat, no cattle."

Occasionally, you might find an important morsel of information on these message boards. Back in the mid '90s, we followed a small company based in Alexandria, Louisiana, called Rankin Automotive. The Internet was just coming into its own. We met with an executive in their conference room, and he opened with a friendly, "What do you know?" One of my students took the question literally and said, "I know you're going to open a new distribution facility in Monroe, Louisiana, and the announcement will be Monday at 9 a.m. I read it on the Internet."

This information had not yet been circulated by the company, but the executive bit his lip, recognized that the Internet was here to stay, and smirked, "Ha, they got the time wrong!" That to me was an "aha moment." The future of business information and stock research "was a-changing."

If the company you're following operates in your region, ask around at work, church, civic organizations, and the like. I'm always amazed at how easy it is to connect with someone knowledgeable about the company. Not only is this a great way to find out how business is going, you can often learn about the culture and whether people actually enjoy working there.

Every industry has a trade association. I was giving a talk in Washington, D.C., a few years back, and noticed that the directory of tenants next to the elevator included a listing for the Association of Associations. Oh, brother! Each association will have a public relations officer who is more than happy to provide a background on the industry as well as the challenges, opportunities, and trends facing the business. This can be a gold mine.

Our Burkenroad students aren't shy. They often contact the company's competitors, suppliers, and customers. We have found a lot of good information here. And remember that most people like to talk about their work, and they like to talk about themselves. Companies that seem to be in mundane businesses are fascinating in their own way. The questions you ask should indicate that you've done your homework. And finally, be respectful of their time. Promise these busy people that you're only going to take a few minutes of their time...and hold to it.

And frankly, there's a certain satisfaction you get from asking your own questions and doing your own research. Do it yourself. As the saying goes, "Give a man a fish and he eats for just one day, give a fish a man and he eats for like two and a half months!" Well... it's something like that.

16

Taking Names

The students enjoy our company site visits. For some undergraduates, it's their first business trip. Little do they know how tiring this business travel will eventually get! I travel a lot to give speeches, and after a couple of days on the road, I'm generally worn out and my clothes have been refolded so often they look like origami! Recently, I was with a team of students traveling through the Houston International Airport. Everyone was dressed in their finest, and the shoeshine man yelled out to us, "Can't be making deals with dirty heels!" We all laughed, and two of us signed up for a shine!

Having this armada of sharp, eager, and enthusiastic business students is great, and being an academic program gives us an edge when it comes to objectively researching public companies. The program, however, does have one big disadvantage versus Wall Street—graduation gives us a 100 percent annual turnover of personnel!

I enjoy getting to know my students on our site visits. I'll never forget the student who told me how, as an undergraduate, he and his buddy would go into town and sometimes enjoy themselves a bit too much. Knowing the serious perils of driving while impaired, they would walk to the local pizzeria, order, and asked to be delivered home with the pizza. Young people, they're problem solvers!

I hear folks dismiss this generation as spoiled, insufferable, and unmotivated, but I think that's 180 degrees off. Since 1986, I have taught more than 5,500 Tulane students. They have been wonderful, and it's been a lot of fun. The students with whom I am working are smart, driven, ethical, and community-minded. After Hurricane Katrina, Tulane president Scott Cowen created a mandatory "service learning" requirement that sends our students off to tutor elementary schoolers, gut houses, or whatever else is needed in the New Orleans area. In stock market parlance, "Don't sell them short." America is very fortunate to have such a great generation coming up.

Low-Level Police Work

Among many other factors, I grade my students on their independent outside research. They have lots of ideas and are really good at turning over rocks. This is often called "channel checking" and involves talking to customers, suppliers, and competitors. They can't be just regurgitating what they heard from management or found on the Internet. I think that the readers of our reports really value this extra, unusual effort.

For example, we follow a company called Marine Products Corporation (MPX), out of Atlanta. Marine Products is one of the top four manufacturers of standard-drive powerboats in the United States. Their Robalo sportfishing boats are very big here in Louisiana. (Hey, our license plates say "Sportsman's Paradise.") The boat business is driven by consumer confidence. You really need people to feel OK about their jobs and their economic future to get them to shell out money for a big ticket luxury item like a boat.

In the winter of 2012, five of my students went with clipboards to the New Orleans Boat Show. They went around asking people, "Are you in the market for a boat?" and "Why now?"

A lot of people said they'd been wanting a new boat, but the way the economy had been they'd been reluctant to buy one. That year, though, they'd brought their checkbooks to the event. As it turned out, this was valuable information, as both revenues and the stock price soon began to rise. That April, the company announced a 54% increase in boat sales for the first quarter.

Others said their existing boat was very old and needed repairs, and they were just on the cusp of having to replace it.

The students also hung around outside the Marine Products booth, asking visitors what they thought of the company's current line of boats. That's the kind of information they brought to their reports.

Model Building

A company reports its earnings four times a year. You'll notice that management will compare the current quarter's results to the same quarter last year. This takes the seasonality factors out and gives investors and analysts a more "apples to apples" comparison. Alone, the earnings per share doesn't tell you if people are disappointed or enthused. As a rule of thumb, if analyst expectations were higher than what was reported, the stock drops. If analyst expectations were lower than actual results, then the stock goes up. Analysts are paying particular attention to the company's "forward-looking statements" to help them adjust their models.

Once we were over at the facilities of egg distributor Cal-Maine. One of my students had his laptop open—which actually I discourage during visits, but anyway—there were lots of columns and rows on the screen, all different colors. The CFO looked over my student's shoulder and said, "What's that?" The student said, "It's the financial model we created for the company." The CFO just laughed, and drawled: "My model is pretty much the price of eggs minus price of feed."

The students spend hours with the ever-patient Professor Anthony Wood, who provides the framework to help the students build the essential financial models for each company. It's a lot of work! We push these forecasting and modeling abilities because we think that's what helps to separate our students from others seeking positions at top investment firms.

17

Plant and See

Yes, what we do at Burkenroad Reports takes an enormous amount of work, and it costs about $750,000 per year to run the program. But you can replicate some of the best parts by forming an investment club dedicated to underfollowed public companies in your region.

Fifteen years ago, more than 400,000 people were in investment clubs. Now there are just 39,000. That's a 90 percent decline! These once-popular investment clubs were where friends gathered to talk stocks and pool their money to purchase them. The clubs and their fellowship have faded away. As a contrarian, that tells me now is a great time to start one. Here are my suggestions.

Ten Good Ideas

1. Find some people who really want to learn more about the stock market.

2. Go to www.betterinvesting.com, a site sponsored by the non-profit National Association of Investors Corporation (NAIC). They have some great materials available on how to correctly set up an investment club and avoid the legal and personality issues that can doom a group.

3. Find several public companies in your area that have been over-looked by Wall Street. Your local newspaper probably lists local companies in their Sunday issue. They may include big out-of-state companies operating in the area, but focus on the ones actually headquartered in your region.

BLOOMBERG LOUISIANA

Company	Close	% Change 1D	% Change 1Yr	$1k Inv 1Yr	Company	Close	% Change 1D	% Change 1Yr	$1k Inv 1Yr
Albemarie	64.69	2.1	8.8	1104.12	LamarAdv	44.18	-0.6	58.4	1583.51
Amedisys	10.92	2.4	-14.2	858.49	LHC Group	19.6	-0.9	15.6	1155.66
AT&T	35.6	0.1	0.2	1052.02	LockhdMrtn	109.57	0.4	25.4	1313.94
Atmos En	41.43	1	15.9	1202.51	LouisnaBcp	17.56	1.9	11.4	1114.21
Bristw Grp	68.05	0.7	64	1665.31	MarathonOl	36.37	1.5	48.1	1513.39
Cap One	65.53	0	20.8	1218.66	McDermott	8.71	2.6	-22.6	773.53
CenturyLnk	35.39	0.1	-10.5	957.36	MidsouBcp	16.27	0.4	11.3	1134.39
Chevron	123.27	1.7	18	1219.13	Murphy Oil	62.65	1.4	31.2	1339.64
ChrchlDwn	83.01	0.1	37.2	1388.01	NewparkRes	12.16	2.5	93.3	1933.23
Cleco Corp	47.42	1.3	11.6	1150.74	NortrpGrmn	85.53	0.5	35.5	1389.01
DomRes	57.34	0.8	6.6	1110.69	Petroquest	4.53	-1.1	-14	859.58
Dow Chem	34.02	2.8	9.1	1135.9	Pool Corp	54.27	0.5	33.5	1355.53
Entergy	69.14	0.3	1.7	1067.93	RegionsFin	10.2	0.5	53.8	1549.83
EPL Oil&G	31.21	0.7	79.3	1792.65	RylDutch A	64.56	1.1	-4.1	1008.9
ExxonMobil	93.34	1.2	11.6	1145.49	SandrsnFm	70.57	2.4	60.6	1628.92
FreeprtMcM	27.64	0.7	-17.2	857.53	StewartEnt	13.18	0	70.9	1745.2
Globalstar	0.62	-2.2	112	2120.48	Stone En	23.59	1.8	-7.3	926.55
GulfIsland	21.5	1.6	-27.1	741.66	SuperiorEn	28.01	2.4	37.6	1375.74
Hancock	32.04	0.6	4.2	1075.7	Teche	43.5	-1.1	11.5	1145.69
Home Bcp	18.47	0.3	7.3	1072.59	Textron	26.89	2.2	11.2	1115.39
HornbckOff	57.66	0.8	45.2	1452.39	Tidewater	58.37	1.6	23.6	1262
Iberiabank	56.2	0.2	12.7	1158.42	W&T Offshr	15.37	1.7	2.4	1045.88
JPMorg Ch	54.89	0.3	61.6	1661.49					

The Times-Picayune - Wednesday, July 10, 2013

4. Assign each member to research one company using some of the techniques offered in this book. Have them report their findings to the group, and take a vote on whether to purchase shares in the company.

5. Start your research by reading the company's 10-K, an annual document required by the Securities and Exchange Commission. Like other essential shareholder information, it's found on the company's website. While the annual report can be attractive and glossy, what you need to understand the company is right in the 10-K. Two sections are must-reads. The "business" section discusses things like the company's main products and services, regulations, labor conditions, competitors, and seasonality. The "risk factor" section discusses risks uniquely facing the company as well as more general ones, such as industry risks, economic risks, and regional risks. For instance, companies in our part of the world often have a mention of hurricane risk.

6. Ideally, you should end up with a well-monitored, diversified portfolio of under-followed public companies in your area. Keep in mind that, held alone, these kinds of stocks are often very volatile. That's why you hope to own about a dozen or more of these stocks in your portfolio. I believe one reason the Burkenroad Mutual Fund has done well is that it usually holds about 50 different stocks, representing several industries, at any one time. Diversifying can help take the sting out of the inevitable stock-picking mistakes, such as I described in Chapter 8, "Lessons Learned."

7. It may even be possible to have someone from the company come in and address your group. Overlooked companies are often eager to tell their stories. Hey, if you play your cards right, you may even get a site visit to some of the companies!

8. Like ending a relationship, it's sometimes very difficult to let go of a stock. Before buying a stock, the group should clearly know why it's being acquired and what the stock's target is. When the story has changed or the target has been reached, the group needs to reevaluate the holding. I have kept a diary of my stock trades, and looking back on the rationale and the results has taught me a lot.

9. I suggest that you consider this rather humble approach to building your positions in these stocks. Nobody knows the short-term direction of the market, so if you wanted to own 1,000 shares of the company, you might buy 500 shares initially. This helps create a positive psychology. If the shares go down, you can feel good about the opportunity to add to your holdings at a lower price. If the price rises, you can bask in your success in owning the original low-priced shares.

10. You can even come up with pithy titles for your reports. This is a good exercise in creativity and has always been one of the favorite parts of report writing for my students. One team titled their report on the chicken processor Sanderson Farms "Poultry in Motion." I had to edit others: For example, a group of students covering Stone Energy (SGY) thought "Everybody Must

Get Stone" would be a title that would in some way honor the song while getting a giggle from readers.

And some I still laugh about. While visiting the warehouse facility for ceiling fan and lighting designer Craftmade International (after a roller coaster ride in its stock prices, the company was bought out in 2010 by Litex Corporation), an MBA student asked Craftmade's CEO if ceiling fans had different degrees of horsepower. He responded by telling us that the ceiling fan in his bedroom was so powerful, it could "suck the sheets off the bed!" The students remembered this line when they completed their report and titled it "Craftmade International: When the Sheets Hit the Fan!"

I have addressed many investment clubs over the years, and one of my all-time favorites is an all-male investment club in Shreveport, Louisiana, called "The Syndicate." (I mention this only because a great many of the clubs I've worked with have been made up mostly of women.) About 50 members have been meeting and investing (and enjoying some very fine dinners) for 55 years. Heck, they even have their own flag. It's blue with gold dollar signs and some Latin that translates to "I've been rich and I've been poor, and rich is better." They won't get any arguments from me!

Let's Create an Arena for Ideas

We have created a link on our website, www.stocksunderrocks.com, which will serve as a virtual water cooler where readers can gather with their "stocks under rocks" ideas. Tell us about a stock you've found, and maybe our students will include it in our Burkenroad Reports research.

We are looking for any public company with these general parameters:

- An equity market cap of between $50 million and $2 billion
- Profitable in at least two of the past three years
- Five or fewer analysts following the stock*

All of this information is readily available on the Internet: Just check the company's website under "Investor Relations."

Write to us and tell us how you found this company and why you think it would make a good investment. Don't forget to tell us a little bit about yourself, your interest in the stock market, and your investment strategy.

I think you'll find that searching around under those "rocks" is a lot of fun—and it can be very profitable as well.

KEEP DIGGING.

---

* You can find this information at either the company's website under "investor relations" or at www.cnbc.com by looking up the company's stock quote and checking under the earnings tab.

18

When You're Lost, Everything's a Sign

Investing is all about gathering, interpreting, and acting on reliable information. As I list some of my favorite sources of investing information and opinions, I'm reminded of this quote from Cicero: "I wonder that a soothsayer doesn't laugh whenever he sees another soothsayer."

Here are some sources we rely on.

Recommended Readings

Popular Books

One Up on Wall Street, Peter Lynch

A Zebra in Lion's Country, Ralph Wanger

The Money Masters, John Train

The Little Book That Beats the Street, Joel Greenblatt

Analytical Books

The Intelligent Investor, Benjamin Graham

Security Analysis, Benjamin Graham and David Dodd

Sophisticated and Well Written

Common Sense and Uncommon Profits, Phillip Fisher

The Contrarian Investment Strategy, David Dreman

Investing Websites

Investopedia.com

Bloomberg.com

MotleyFool.com

NPR.org/blogs/money/ (NPR's Planet Money feature)

Seeking Alpha.com

Wikinvest.com

YahooFinance.com

Insightful Investing Experts and Newsletters

Jeremy Grantham, GMO, www.gmo.com

Howard Marks, Oaktree Capital, www.oaktreecapital.com

Bill Nasgowitz, Heartland Funds, www.heartlandfunds.com

Jim Paulsen, Wells Capital Management, www.wellscap.com

Jason Desena Trennert, Strategas, www.strategasrp.com

Here is a list of the public companies the students follow at Burkenroad Reports. It's rather fluid. For the most current coverage universe, visit our website at www.burkenroad.org.

Burkenroad Reports
2013-2014 Companies Under Coverage

COMPANY	SYMBOL/EXCHANGE	INDUSTRY	HEADQUARTERS
AFC Enterprises	AFCE/NASDAQ	Restaurants	Atlanta, GA
Amerisafe	AMSF/NASDAQ	Insurance	DeRidder, LA
BRISTOW GROUP	BRS/NYSE	Offshore Helicopter Services	Houston, TX
Callon Petroleum Company	CPE/NYSE	Oil & Gas Exploration	Natchez, MS
Cal-Maine Foods	CALM/NASDAQ	Food Processing – Eggs	Jackson, MS
Carbo Ceramics	CRR/NYSE	Oilfield Services	Irving, TX
Cash America	CSH/NYSE	Pawn Shops	Ft.Worth, TX
CLECO Corporation	CNL/NYSE	Regional Utility	Pineville, LA
Conn's Inc.	CONN/NASDAQ	Retailing	Houston, TX
Conrad Industries, Inc.	CNRD.PK	Marine Construction & Repair	Morgan City, LA
Crown Crafts Inc.	CRWS/NASDAQ	Juvenile Goods	Gonzales, LA
Cyberonics Inc.	CYBX/NASDAQ	Medical Equipment	Houston, TX
Denbury Resources	DNR/NYSE	Oil & Gas Exploration	Plano, TX
EastGroup Properties	EGP/NYSE	Real Estate	Jackson, MS
EPL Oil & Gas Inc.	EPL/NYSE	Oil & Gas Exploration	New Orleans, LA
Evolution Petroleum	EPM/NYSE•AMEX	Oil & Gas Exploration	Houston, TX
Gulf Island Fabrication	GIFI/NASDAQ	Oilfield Services	Houma, LA
Hibbett Sports	HIBB/NASDAQ	Sporting Goods	Birmingham, AL
Hornbeck Offshore Services	HOS/NYSE	Oilfield Services	Covington, LA
Houston Wire and Cable	HWCC/NASDAQ	Electrical Equipment	Houston, TX
IBERIABANK Corporation	IBKC/NASDAQ	Banking	New Iberia, LA
ION Geophysical Corporation	IO/NYSE	Oilfield Services	Stafford, TX
Key Energy Services	KEG/NYSE	Oilfield Services	Houston, TX
Marine Products Corporation	MPX/NYSE	Consumer Goods – Boats	Atlanta, GA
MidSouth Bancorp	MSL/NYSE•AMEX	Banking	Lafayette, LA
PetroQuest Energy	PQ/NYSE	Oil & Gas Exploration	Lafayette, LA
Pool Corporation	POOL/NASDAQ	Pool Products	Covington, LA
Powell Industries	POWL/NASDAQ	Electrical Equipment	Houston, TX
Rollins Inc.	ROL/NYSE	Consumer Services	Atlanta, GA
RPC Inc.	RES/NYSE	Oilfield Services	Atlanta, GA
Sanderson Farms	SAFM/NASDAQ	Food Processing – Chicken	Laurel, MS
Seacor Holdings	CKH/NYSE	Oilfield Services	Houston, TX
Sharps Compliance	SMED/NASDAQ	Medical Waste	Houston, TX
Stone Energy Corporation	SGY/NYSE	Oil & Gas Exploration	Lafayette, LA
Superior Energy Services	SPN/NYSE	Oilfield Services	Harvey, LA
Susser Holdings Corporation	SUSS/NASDAQ	Convenience Stores	Corpus Christi, TX
Susser Petroleum	SUSP/NASDAQ	Fuel Retailing	Corpus Christi, TX
Team Inc.	TISI/NYSE•AMEX	Industrial Services	Alvin, TX
Teche Holding Company	TSH/NYSE	Banking	Franklin, LA
Willbros Group	WG/NYSE	Oilfield Services	Houston, TX

Index

Q

questions, asking, 121-125

R

Regulation Fair Disclosure, 122
repeat business, 55-61
    Cyberonics, 59-61
    POOLCORP, 55-59
researching public companies
    asking questions, 121-125
    student research methods, 127-129
Rollins, Inc., 26-27
RPC, Inc., 117-118

S

Sanderson Farms, 83-86
Sarbanes-Oxley Act, 95
SEACOR, 75-80
share buybacks, 18, 44-45
shareholders, management as, 20
Sharps Compliance, 52-54
short selling, 88
short-term traders, 8-12
small cap stocks
    advantages of, 18-21
        buyout potential, 21
        clean balance sheets, 21
        growth brings attention, 19
        liquidity discount, 19-20
        management as shareholders, 20
        management flexibility, 20
        scale of changes, 18
        share buybacks, 18
    capitalization explained, 16-18
starting investment clubs, 131-134
Stewart Enterprises, 30-31
stock valuation
    catalysts, 115
    EV/EBITDA, 117-118
    P/E ratio, 111-115
    PEG ratio, 115-117
    what to look for, 120

stock-picking
    "Dartboard Stock Picking Contest"
        (Wall Street Journal), 105
    Jim Cramer, 106-107
    lost art of, 109-110
    Warren Buffett, 107-109
stocks. *See also* public companies
    Efficient Market Hypothesis, 10
    insider trading, 46-47
    market capitalization, 16-18
    myths about, 99-103
    overlooked stocks. *See* overlooked
        stocks
    percentage to invest in, 6
    share buybacks, 44-45
    small cap stocks. *See* small cap stocks
    suggesting to Burkenroad Reports,
        134-135
    supply and demand, 96-97
student research methods, 127-129
supply and demand, 96-97
Susser Holdings, 28-29

T

Team, Inc., 38-40
Teche Holdings, 41-44
10-K documents, 132
trailing P/E, 112

U

unemployment rate, effect on stock
    market, 102-103

V

value investing. *See* stock valuation

W

Willbros Group, 49-51

FINANCIAL TIMES

In an increasingly competitive world, it is quality
of thinking that gives an edge—an idea that opens new
doors, a technique that solves a problem, or an insight
that simply helps make sense of it all.

We work with leading authors in the various arenas
of business and finance to bring cutting-edge thinking
and best-learning practices to a global market.

It is our goal to create world-class print publications
and electronic products that give readers
knowledge and understanding that can then be
applied, whether studying or at work.

To find out more about our business
products, you can visit us at www.ftpress.com.